DEBENHAM & FREEBODY'S
SALE
commences Monday July 10
EXCEPTIONAL BARGAINS
IN ALL DEPARTMENTS
The undermentioned are typical examples:

GOWN, in check zephyr, bodice trimmed plain strappings, fully collar and cuffs of fine tucked lawn in various colorings. **Sale price, 18/9**

LINEN SUIT (as sketch) in white linen, braided and trimmed, with a mauve collar. **Special price, 39/6**

SILK NINON WRAP, trimmed with silk embroidery and fringe. **Special Sale Price:** In Black . . . . **52/6** In Grey, Mauve & White, **55/-**

FOULARD GOWN in good quality. Black and white, white and black, mauve and grey, coloured figured foulards, turn-down collar, finished with bow at neck. **49/6**

HOLIDAY COAT (as sketch) in heavy-weight natural Shantung silk, perfectly tailored, and trimmed with a black satin collar. **Special Sale price, 3 gns.**

NORFOLK SUIT (as sketch), made in new autumn tweeds, perfect cut and tailored, coat lined with silk. **Special Sale price, 69/6**

LINEN GOWN (as sketch), in good quality soft finished linen, plain shirt bodice, box pleated, with turn-down collar and cuffs of lawn, and finished with black satin tie. In White, Black, Grey, Mauve and Colours. Usual price, 49/6 **Sale price, 39/6**

PRINTED NINON GOWN over satin, cut with tight skirt, showing band of plain satin at foot, turn-down printed collar of fine lace in black and white and mauve and white printed ninons in spot and small figure designs. **7½ gns.**

SALE CATALOGUE POST FREE.

DEBENHAM & FREEBODY,
Wigmore Street, London, W.

OF
COURSE
A
WOMAN
WANTS
TO
KNOW
THE

DAINTIEST

PERFUMES

HERE
ARE
THREE
OF
THEM.
HAVE
YOU
TRIED
THEM?

A newly-invented apparatus for ladies, each 12/6
,, ,, ,, gentlemen ,, 12/6

Things A Woman Wants to Know

Wants to Know

An Edwardian Housewife's Guide to Life

· OLD HOUSE ·

Published in Great Britain in 2014 by Old House Books,
PO Box 883, Oxford OX1 9PL, UK
PO Box 3985, New York, NY 10185-3985 USA
Website: www.oldhousebooks.co.uk

© 2013 Old House
First published 2013; reprinted 2014.

A CIP catalogue record for this book is available from the
British Library.

This is a compilation of extracts from genuine advice manuals published
between 1890 and 1920. The majority of text was included in *Things A
Woman Wants To Know*, first published in 1901 by C. A. Pearson Ltd,
London.

ISBN-13: 978 1 90840 263 9

Edited by Sarah Marquis.

Cover image: Artwork by Coles Phillips, featured on the cover of
Good Housekeeping Magazine, 1915 (source: MagazineArt.org)

Illustrations are acknowledged as follows:
Amoret Tanner/Alamy, page 15; Beryl Peters Collection/Alamy,
page 62; The Bridgeman Art Library, pages 169 and 170; Jeff Morgan
07/Alamy, pages 23, 54 and 64; Lordprice Collection/Alamy, pages 30
and 49; Mary Evans Picture Library, pages i , 6, 32, 72, 108, 115 and 172;
Topfoto, pages 9, 11, 19, 20, 25, 40, 46, 75, 79, 134 and 136.

Printed in China through World Print Ltd.

14 15 16 17 18   11 10 9 8 7 6 5 4 3 2

Things A Woman Wants to Know

An Edwardian Housewife's Guide to Life

Contents

CHAPTER ONE

Keeping up Appearances

 ## THE TOILETTE

THE woman who pretends to be indifferent to her toilette is wanting in good sense. It is not enough to be a good wife and mother in order to retain the affections of your husband, the father of your children: you must also be an attractive and pleasant woman. However ideally pretty or ideally graceful you may be, you cannot escape some fatal absurdities at certain moments of your toilette. For instance: a woman in the act of curling her hair will not appear to advantage, and may even look ridiculous. Let us wrap the facts of life in some little mystery. It is unnecessary to remind those who hold us dear that though we are goddesses at some times, we are but ordinary women at others.

In the Bathroom, beside the actual baths, there should be a couch or ottoman, whereon to repose after the bath; a little table and a chair, in case one would wish to have a cup of tea. It is unnecessary to place a dressing-table in the bathroom: one returns to one's dressing-room to complete the toilette.

It would be Distinctly Dangerous to take a bath immediately after having eaten. Even minor ablutions are apt to trouble the digestion and one should allow three hours to elapse between any meal and a bath.

On Sea-Bathing. It is best to go rapidly into the water, so that the whole body may be immersed in as short a time

as possible, care being taken, however, to cover up the hair carefully, as there is nothing so disastrous in effect to a woman's hair as sea-water.

Perfume Reveals Character. Scents may be used in moderation, but both health and good taste forbid their being over-done. They are also supposed to have a certain effect on the mind. Musk produces sensitiveness; geranium tenderness; benzoin dreaminess; dark-blue violets predispose to piety; white ones facilitate digestion.

 Raspberry lips. Many women bite their lips on entering a room, to make them red. But, besides the fact that the colour thus obtained only lasts a few seconds, the habit of biting the lips makes them sore and inclined to chap.

Extravagant Laughter on all occasions, for everything and nothing, must not be indulged in by those who wish to keep their lips pretty. Excessive laughter and contortions of the face will disfigure the mouth and bring on premature old age.

Redness of the Nose often proceeds from a kind of congestion. In this case it should be washed with warm water only, on going to bed at night. Such persons must also abstain from ham, or pork under any form.

Diminishing the Size of the Nose. The science of rhinoplasty has made such progress that it is possible now to modify, even to change, the shape of the nose. I may, however, suggest to persons afflicted with a large nose the means of diminishing its size. To do this, it will be sufficient to wear a *pince-nez*, without glasses in it, at night, and in the day-time whenever you are alone.

For Tired Feet after Dancing. Soak your feet in salt and water, and you will feel none of the troubles attendant on tired feet the day after the ball.

Cucumbers are invaluable as an adjunct to the toilet. They should be eaten plentifully by those who have highly coloured complexions. Cucumber-juice *well rubbed into the skin of the face* will keep it clear, fresh, and soft.

A Slice of Lemon passed over the face instead of washing it will cleanse the skin and make it firm and white. It should be used daily. If the skin is too delicate to stand it without feeling sore, lemon-juice may be mixed with equal parts of cream for a lotion.

To free the Hands from Disagreeable Odours. Ground mustard, mixed with a little water, is an excellent agent for

cleansing the hands after handling disagreeable or strongly odorous substances, such as cod liver oil, musk, valerianic acid and its salts. Scale-pans and vessels may also be readily freed from odour by the same method.

To Whiten and Soften the Skin a mixture of equal parts of lemon-juice and cream is very useful, and several society beauties never use any other cosmetic. Lemon Cream for whitening the skin, may be made as follows: Melt together two teaspoonfuls of spermaceti and one ounce of oil of almonds. As it cools, stir in sixteen drops of essence of lemon.

Dandelion for the Complexion. The young leaves should be eaten as a salad, or the root of the dandelion may be bruised and the juice squeezed out and mixed in the proportion of two-thirds juice to one-third of rectified spirits of wine. It should then stand for a week and afterwards be filtered through blotting-paper and a flannel bag. A teaspoonful is to be taken occasionally two or three times a day.

Stains on the Hands may be removed by rubbing them with a little salt moistened with a little lemon-juice, and then washing with clean water and soap.

To Make the Hands Plump. Rub them with sweet oil night and morning. Exercise them by rubbing gently together whenever you have an opportunity. *Never wear tight sleeves or a too-well-fitting glove*, and always keep the arms and hands as warm as possible.

If your Hands are Rather Fat, do not wear tight sleeves.

How to Avoid Growing Stout. Exercise is one of the most esteemed means of bringing the body to reasonable proportions – fatigue should not be feared. Rouse yourselves, ye unfortunate fat ones, for indeed I pity you! Labour till you bring the sweat to your brow.

Excessive Thinness is sometimes joined to an unpleasant temper. You should lead a quiet life, with as few emotions as possible; amuse yourself in your own home. Take tepid baths, and keep cheerful.

Bathing the Eyes several times a day in cold water makes them bright, and preserves the sight to very old age.

A RECIPE FOR CLEANING DELICATE TEETH.

Phosphate of *dry chalk* . . . . . . 2 ounces
Iris Powder. . . . . 1 ounce
Powdered myrrh . . . . 8 grains

Mix these and add:
Solution of *cocaine* . . . . 1 drop
Eucalyptus oil . . . . 12 drops

Mix and heat them well together, and strain. This powder is very good for delicate teeth and spongy gums.

Good Tooth-Powder. Precipitated chalk one ounce, carbonate of soda half an ounce, and the same quantity of powdered orris-root. Pound all together and pass through sieve; then put into pots for use.

Hard Water. When unable to procure soft water for toilet purposes, keep a muslin bag with fine oatmeal in it, and squeeze out in water before washing. Put fresh oatmeal every day.

A Soothing Powder which will remain on the skin is the following:
Boracic acid . . . . 1 part.
Oxide of zinc . . . . 1 part.
Powdered starch . . . . 4 parts.

Preparing a Bath. This is a useful hint, and by its careful practice the enamel of a bath will be preserved in good condition three times as long as usual. In pouring in water for a hot bath always put about half as much cold water as you think will be required, then pour in the hot.

Towels used for the face should be very fine. Rough ones should never be employed, as they are apt to break the tiny blood-vessels in the skin.

ERADICATING IMPERFECTIONS

To Prevent Lines Forming on the Face. After bathing with warm water and drying the face, rub it all over with the ball of the thumb. This stimulates the circulation and strengthens the muscles. If there are deep lines running from the corners of the mouth to the corners of the nose, lay the thumb along them, and then work it from side to side.

Ulcerated eruptions have been cured by bathing with strawberry-juice. It is much less repugnant than, and quite as efficacious as, a *live yellow slug*, with which the sore used to be rubbed till the unhappy mollusc was used up.

Redness in the Hands. Beat together an ounce of clear honey, one ounce of almond oil, the juice of a lemon, and the yolk of a raw egg. Apply at night to the hands, and cover with old gloves slit up in the palms.

Sty in the Eye. Take a piece of *hot baked apple*, wrap it in muslin, apply it to the eye; keep it in its place by binding a handkerchief round the head. This should be done at night and the sty will be greatly lessened, if not quite gone, by the morning.

Treatment of Bunions. Put some *large ivy leaves* into a cupful of vinegar, and, after soaking some hours, place carefully over the bunion. Change once or twice a day, always being careful to choose a leaf fresh out of the vinegar. This is excellent for corns. Another good way to treat bunions is to paint them every second day with tincture of iodine.

Castor Oil rubbed into warts two or three times a day will generally cure them, but if not they may be safely cured by keeping them damp with a rag dipped in vinegar, slicing them thinly day by day, and applying powdered alum to the fresh surface.

A Poultice of Stale Bread soaked in strong vinegar applied on retiring will relieve corns.

Blistered Feet. Soaping the inside of the stocking with a thick lather before setting out for a long walk will prevent the feet from blistering. When hard walking is intended, good, well-fitting, well-greased boots should be selected; a *raw egg broken into the boots* before putting them on softens the leather to a great extent. When you have been some hours on the road, and the feet begin to be chafed, change your stockings or turn them inside out. Should a blister be formed, mix a little tallow from your bedroom candle with spirit on going to bed, in the palm of your hand, and rub your feet with it. In the morning the blister will have gone.

Perspiration of the Hands is often due to constitutional causes, and a strong tonic of iron and quinine should be taken. For excessive perspiration of the hands and under the arms the following is a very useful powder:—

Oxide of zinc . . . . 1 ounce.
Powdered starch . . . . 4 ounces.

Mix, and keep constantly applied.

Those who have Weak Eyebrows and Lashes can strengthen the growth and darken the colour by the use of cocoa butter, which should be applied at bedtime.

When Hair in the Eyebrows is scanty a little *benzoated lard* may be applied to them every night and morning.

In applying this it should be put on with the forefinger, moving it gently from the nose towards the outer corner of the eye, and all the hairs should be smoothed neatly in the semicircular shape of an ideal eyebrow.

No Face Powder should be used that is insoluble in water, for if ordinary rice, starch, or chalk powders are used it is impossible quite to free the skin from them by ordinary washing, and the little pores become clogged.

To Avoid Chapped Hands. Take common starch and grind it with a knife until it is reduced to the finest powder, put in a clean tin box, so as to have it continually at hand for use. After washing your hands, rinse them thoroughly in clean water, wipe them, and while they are yet damp, rub a pinch of the starch thoroughly over them, covering the whole surface. The effect is magical. The rough, smarting skin is cooled and healed.

To Whiten the Hands. Mix thoroughly eau de Cologne, two ounces; lemon-juice, two ounces; powdered brown Windsor soap, six ounces. When hard it will be an excellent soap for whitening the hands.

In Cases of Eczema the method of applying hot steam to the parts has been attended with success in many cases. The steam is applied for periods varying from a quarter to half an hour. It removes the crusts easily, and encourages the healing of the hard surfaces, which can then be treated by the ordinary remedies.

An Excellent Lotion for Wrinkles is made of: Thick milk of almonds, two ounces; rose-water, eight ounces; sulphate of aluminia, one and a quarter drachms.

To Remove Freckles. Take one ounce of lemon-juice, quarter of a drachm of borax, powdered, and a half-drachm of sugar. Mix well and let it stand in a bottle for three days, and it will be fit for use, and should be rubbed on the face and hands occasionally.

Growing Old Gracefully. Take more pains than ever with your person. If you neglect any of the little habits of neatness, decrepitude will come on all the faster.

HAIRCARE FOR LADIES

To Clean Combs. If it can be avoided *never wash combs*, as the water very often makes the teeth split, and renders the tortoiseshell or horn of which they are made rough. Small brushes manufactured for the purpose of cleaning combs may be purchased at a trifling cost; with one of these the comb should be well brushed, and afterwards wiped with a cloth or towel.

Combing and Rubbing the Scalp of the head with the hand draws the blood up to the surface of the head, and not only relieves headache, but adds new strength to the hair.

The Use of Hot Irons to curl and crimp the hair is *very harmful*. The heat injures the vitality of the hair and makes it dry and brittle, while the irons pull the hair. The use of curling papers or the lead or leather curlers made for the purpose, is not nearly so bad, and gives quite as good an effect.

The Fashion of Frizzing the Hair, whether with hot irons, pins, or any other artificial means of making it wavy, is a disastrous one for the beauty and growth of the hair.

Falsifying a Fringe. Many women, thinking themselves very clever, wear a false fringe, which opens a new danger. Very often false hair, in spite of the purifying it has undergone, has communicated skin disease to the wearer. Hair taken from the dead is never used by hairdressers who value their reputation – it cannot be frizzed or curled without great difficulty.

Hairwash. Pour a quart of boiling water on a small handful of rosemary, add a *piece of ammonia* the size of a walnut; let it stand till cold, when it will be ready for use. This wash will be found to cleanse the hair and at the same time stimulate its growth.

To Cure Dandruff. Apply sweet almond oil to the scalp every night. Rub it in thoroughly and in the morning shampoo with soap and soft water, rinsing with plenty of cold water.

A good Shampoo Liquid for cleansing the head from dandruff is the following:—

Carbonate of ammonia	1 drachm.
Carbonate of potash	1 drachm.
Water	4 ounces.
Tincture of cantharides	4 drachms.
Alcohol	4 ounces.
Rum	1 ½ pints.

Dissolve the carbonate in the water, and shake well before using. Moisten the scalp well with this until a lather forms. Wash in cold water, and rub.

23

To Stop Hair Falling Out. Wash the head every other day with this mixture, rubbing it hard: *Three common onions* cleaned and put in *a quart of rum* for twenty-four hours; the onions are then taken out, and the rum used to rub the scalp. The slight odour of onions it may retain should evaporate in a few minutes.

To Darken the Hair fill a teacup *half full of tea*, pour boiling water over it, and let it stand for an hour or two; pour off the dark part, and wash the hair with it, applying the mixture with a sponge. It should be used several times at first, and then perhaps once a week to keep the hair dark when fading. Care should be taken not to touch the hands more than can be helped, as it stains them. This is not in any way injurious.

A Hair-Brush may be cleaned by *rubbing with flour*. When quite clean, remove all traces of flour with a dry towel. This method preserves the varnish on the wood and prevents the bristles from becoming soft.

Brilliantine for the Hair. Boil an ounce of quince seeds with a pint and a half of water till reduced to half that quantity, then strain off the liquor, scent it with any essence desired, and bottle for use.

ON DRESS

On slatternly dress. A man will find it much easier to accord the little courtesies of well-bred society to his wife if she is neatly and becomingly dressed, however simple the gown may be, than if she is untidy. The children also will find it much easier to love, honour and obey if their parents give a reasonable amount of time to their personal appearance.

Underclothing. A virtuous woman has a repugnance towards excessive luxury in her underclothing. What can be more refreshing than to put on fresh linen?

In Mature Age, let us put away all pretensions to juvenility. A dowager in a *decolletée* tulle dress, with nothing on her head, is hideous. An octogenarian can still be beautiful and charming, but she should not dress like her granddaughter.

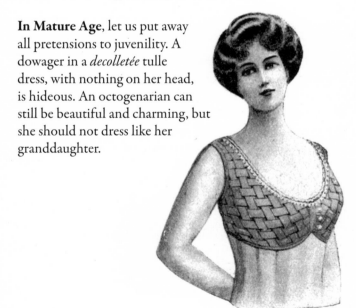

ADVICE TO A STOUT WOMAN.

- She must deny herself bows and rosettes of ribbon at the waist, as this adornment adds to its size.
- She ought not to wear short sleeves, nor a very high collar.
- She ought to dress her hair high up on her head, and the front should not be plastered down.
- Patterns with large flowers, or checks, must be avoided for her dresses. Plain materials are all that she can allow herself, and she should wear dark shades.

No one should Wear a Low Dress who has not a good neck and arms. Sharp shoulder blades and pointed elbows are not pleasant to look at, and are best covered.

PRINCIPLES OF COLOUR.

- *Fair Women* are mistaken in wearing light blue. A rich blue suits them very well, but neutral tints are very unbecoming to them.
- *Brunettes with sallow complexions* should avoid blue altogether. Green is doubtful for them, unless their skin is very white.
- *Pale brunettes* should affect those shades of red which heighten their beauty. Crimson may perhaps be admitted.
- Yellow is a splendid colour for a *pale dark woman.*
- People may say what they like, but yellow is very unbecoming to *blondes.*

SUNDRY HINTS FOR YOUNG LADIES

Never be cast down by Trifles. If a spider breaks his thread twenty times, he will mend it again as often.

If you have Pretty Hands and Arms, you may play on the harp if you play well. If they are disposed to be clumsy, work tapestry.

If you have Good Teeth, do not laugh in order to show them. If you have bad teeth, do not laugh less than the occasion may warrant.

If you have Pretty Feet there is still no occasion to wear short petticoats.

Never Revenge an Injury. If you have an enemy, act kindly to her, and make her your friend.

 ## HINTS FOR WIVES

A Wife's Power. The power of a wife for good or evil is irresistible. Home must be the seat happiness, or it must be forever unknown. If at home a man finds no rest, and is there met with bad temper, or gloom, or is assailed by discontent or complaint, he sinks into despair.

If your Husband appears Troubled, let him alone until he is inclined to talk. Take up your book or your needlework pleasantly and cheerfully. Above all, don't let him find a shirt-button missing.

Never Complain that your husband pores too much over the newspaper. Neither should you hide the paper, but when the boy leaves it at the door, take it in pleasantly and lay it down before him.

DON'T
HUNGER STRIKE,
TAKE
BEECHAM'S
PILLS.

CHAPTER TWO

Medical Matters

WHAT A WOMAN SHOULD WEIGH.

A woman whose height is:—

Ft.	In.	Lbs.	Ft.	In.	Lbs.
5	0	118	5	5	139
5	1	124	5	6	143
5	2	128	5	7	148
5	3	130	5	8	153
5	4	136	5	9	158

This table is for women between twenty and forty-five years of age. After that they become heavier.

 BEWARE!

Many Cases of Indigestion arise from people drinking too much at meals. The solids they take are greatly diluted in this way, and the work of the stomach is hindered. This caution applies equally to water, beer, &c.

In Purchasing Canned Goods it is a safe rule to observe whether the head of the can is concave, a bulging appearance being indicative of decomposition.

Rules for Sleeping. There are two rules for sleeping which everybody may adopt without hesitation. First, *never let yourself be awakened*, but wait until you have slept out your sleep. Second, *get up as soon as you are awake*. If you follow these two rules the hours of sleep will soon regulate themselves to the requirements of your constitution.

To avoid Catching Cold accustom yourself to the use of sponging with cold water every morning on first getting out of bed, followed by a good rubbing with a wet towel. This proves a safeguard against the injurious influence of cold and sudden changes of temperature.

Value of Cream. Those to whom cod liver oil is a necessity, but who cannot take it, will find cream a perfect substitute. People with a consumptive tendency should take it as an antidote. It is excellent for old people, invalids, and those who have feeble digestions.

Drink Water. Nowadays people do not drink enough water to thin the blood, so that the system can be cleared of its effete matter quickly and promptly. The consequence is that the long-continued retention of secretions, which should be thrown off, produces rheumatism and catarrh, and affects the heart. The use of water in its normal quantity keeps the stomach and bowels clean, and really has the effect of an *inside bath*.

Water which is very Bright and sparkling and has a taste (if it is not mineral water) should be looked upon with suspicion. Some of the worst waters, laden with cholera germs and with the germs of other diseases, have been bright, clear waters. It is a mistake to suppose really bad water is necessarily dirty in appearance. Well waters should be regularly analysed. They are apt to become fouled by the surrounding earth, for even a well-built well in time must allow matters to leak into it.

The Effect of Walking, especially if the arms are swung, is to exercise most of the muscles in the body, to raise the temperature, to quicken the breathing and the pulse, increase the action of the skin, improve digestion, and make one hungry.

Stings of Insects. Country life has one great drawback: the unbearable stings of mosquitos or gnats. If you are stung, run into the garden for *a leek or an onion*, and rub the place with it. This is, no doubt, a remedy as heroic as it is excellent.

Another Cure for Stings. Many people use sticks of butter of cocoa as a cosmetic. If *a little cocaine* (2 per cent) be added to it, and the sting rubbed with the stick, it will procure immediate relief.

In the Winter Season remember the necessity which exists for an increase in our fatty foods, and don't neglect the advice to take plenty of fat in cold weather. This is a natural law of diet, and its observance will result in saving us from much illness.

Soiled Linen Bags. On no account keep these in the sleeping apartment, for it is very unhealthy, and tends to taint the air which is inhaled during the night.

Ice taken from ponds, canals, and rivers is highly impure, being a mass of frozen matter; the offensiveness is not destroyed by cold. Before use, ice should be certified to be pure. Similarly, *ice-creams from barrows are dangerous*, owing to the risk of unwashed glasses, and the water and the other materials used in their manufacture not being of the best.

Never Put Money in the Mouth. The act of holding money in the mouth or between the teeth or lips is a thoughtless one, but none the less of the most dangerous kind. Money is handled by *all classes*, goes into and out of houses and families where sickness prevails, and that *disease may often lurk in a bank-note* or on the face of a coin is as probable as it is possible.

When Perspiring do not go into the presence of any contagious disease, nor when the system is not properly fortified with food. Open pores and an empty stomach render one more liable to take the disease.

Damp Beds are most dangerous, and sleeping in a bed that has not been properly aired has often laid the foundation of a severe cold, an attack of rheumatism, &c. A sure test of discovering if the bed be well aired is to put an ordinary hand-glass between the sheets. Leave it for a few minutes, and if, on taking it out, the glass looks misty, it will be wiser to remove the sheets and sleep between the blankets. If, on the contrary, the glass is perfectly clear and unclouded, the bed may be slept in without any fears.

Yawning is generally regarded as a singularly impolite habit. Perhaps it is, socially considered; but, physiologically, yawning has the good effect of clearing the ear-tubes, and of relieving pain in the ears due to excess of wax secretion.

 NURSING THE SICK

Cheerful Amusement is the best cure for many nervous complaints and debility. The stimulus of laughter quickens the circulation and the action of the heart, increases the appetite, and improves all the conditions of life.

Invalid's Pick-me-up. A teaspoonful of brandy in two tablespoonfuls of beef-tea is useful for a patient faint from weakness.

Do not Bother the Sick. Do not bother a sick person when he is doing anything, nor interrupt him when speaking. Furthermore:

- Never lean against, sit upon, or *shake the bed* upon which a sick person lies.
- Never read to the sick except when they ask it; then read what they wish, slowly and distinctly.
- Give a little variety to the room by occasionally changing things. If flowers are liked, get them, but beware of the effect of very sweet perfumes.
- Give a little food at a time, but give often if craved.
- As a rule invalids have slow appetites in the morning. You can sustain them till they get a desire for something substantial by giving them a little beef-tea or light broth.
- Never leave untasted food at the patient's bedside from meal to meal. The sight of that which is not craved is repellent.
- Do not fill a patient's plate. Have tempting quantities temptingly prepared and served. Cook with care.
- As a rule you can afford to give a patient a little of whatever is craved unless the physician forbids it.
- Sometimes the craving is morbid; then you can refuse to gratify it. Carefully watch the bedding. Keep the sheets clean and dry. Change the clothing often. Never let a bed get damp or foul.
- Do not load the patient with bed-clothing.

Milk is the greatest comfort in a serious case of illness, for it is the only diet on which sick people can live without wasting.

Coffee is a fairly good air purifier. A little burned on hot coals will purify a sick-room and abolish bad smells. Many physicians think highly of the bracing effects of coffee, taken before they visit infectious diseases.

When a Person is recovering from a serious chronic disorder, or after an accident or surgical operation, sea-air tends to restore the system far better than either inland or mountain air. In certain nervous complaints, however, and in neuralgia, sea-air has often a bad effect by being *too exciting*, and a mild country air is usually preferable.

Scents for the Sick-Room. In long cases of illness the patient wearies of every kind of scent in turn, and one is so often at a loss what perfume to use. Procure from a chemist a small quantity of oil of sandal-wood. Heat a shovel well, and drop on to it a few drops of the oil. This will at once diffuse a delightful odour through the sick-room, and will be found very refreshing to the patient. Another way of imparting a delightful freshness to a sick-room is by placing a piece of camphor in a saucer and laying on it a red-hot poker. The fumes from the camphor will soon permeate through the room, and cause all closeness to disappear. A simple means of changing the air in a sick-room is to open the window at the top, and opening the door, move it backwards and forwards rapidly, so as to ensure a current of fresh air from the window.

Hot Sand-Bags. These are very useful in sickness, and far more pleasant to use than hot-water bottles. Make a bag of flannel eight or ten inches square, fill it with dry sand, and sew it up. Then put a cotton cover over the flannel—this prevents the sand sifting out, and holds the heat—place the bag in the oven to heat, or put it on the stove. The sand holds the heat a long time, and the bag can be tucked up to the back without hurting a sick person.

HOUSEHOLD REMEDIES FOR UNFORTUNATE CONDITIONS

Flatulent Indigestion. Sufferers should abstain from tea and coffee, and take instead a mixture of three parts of scalded milk to one of lime-water.

Persons with Delicate Feet should give them a brisk rubbing daily with salt and cold water. Those who suffer from perspiration of the feet should wash them daily with soap and water, then sponge them with tepid alum water for a few minutes. This will take off any smell and hardens the skin.

For Simple Hoarseness. Take a fresh egg, beat it, and thicken with pulverised sugar. Eat freely of this, and the hoarseness will soon be relieved.

To Cure Earache. *Roast an onion* in the coals and take out the centre, put the fine point of the *centre into the ear*, and let it remain several hours.

The Best Remedy for Nose Bleeding is one so very simple that you may feel inclined to doubt it. It consists in vigorous motion of the jaws as in the act of mastication. In the case of a child a wad of paper should be placed in its mouth, and the child instructed to chew it hard, but be careful not to swallow it.

Opium a Soothing Balm. Mix two drachms of bruise opium with half a pint of boiling water. Use, when cold, for painful ulcers, bruises, etc.

Insomnia. Pillows stuffed with camel's-hair, and covered with the skin of the same animal, are useful against insomnia. *Inhaling onions* will also aid in encouraging sleep.

For an Acute Attack of Diarrhoea. An excellent remedy is to keep entirely to a diet of hot milk, which is to be taken as hot as it can be swallowed without scalding the lips, as if so, it is likely to scald the gullet and stomach, and set up inflammation.

In Bronchitis and Colds of Winter. Lettuce contains a mild principle of opiate nature called "lettuce-opium." A salad of lettuce at night may therefore be regarded as a homely and safe enough remedy for sleeplessness of a mild nature.

For a Cough. Boil together, stirring to prevent burning, half a cup of treacle, and a piece of butter the size of a walnut; squeeze into this the juice of one lemon; this is a simple and often an effective remedy for an ordinary cough.

DIFFERENT KINDS OF BATHS.

There are various kinds of baths specially suited to various occasions.

- For rheumatism, pour a little turpentine into the water.
- For sleeplessness, rub with alcohol after drying.
- For softening the skin, drop a bag filled with almond meal or bran into the water, and use it as a rubber.
- For sweetness, pure and simple, a dash of rose, lily, or heliotrope is good, or a little lavender-water. Bags of bruised lavender may also be thrown into the water.

Buttermilk is a good remedy for vomiting arising from irritability of the stomach and other causes. Hot water – really hot, not tepid – has also a wonderfully soothing action on the stomach. It should be sipped slowly.

For Sickness suck ice, and *lay it on the back of the neck.*

Hiccough is a troublesome, even if a simple affection, although it may be a very bad sign indeed, in cases of actual disease. To prevent it, a good remedy is to close the ears with the index fingers, and then to swallow a small quantity of liquid, presented by another person to the patient.

A Remedy for Offensive Breath, which arise from stomach disorder, is given as follows (the food, of course, is also to be considered, all acids, sweets, pastry, cheese, and the like being avoided):—

Carbonate of bismuth . . . . . 10 grains.
Wood charcoal . . . . .10 grains
Bicarbonate of soda . . . . 5 grains

Mix. One such powder to be taken thrice a day, half an hour before meals, when acidity, *&c*, is present.

Those who Suffer from Constipation will find linseed tea very useful. A teacupful of boiling water may be poured on a tablespoonful of linseed. This should be allowed to stand for an hour, and the whole should then be taken fasting.

For the Brain-Worker. The best time for physical exercise is in the afternoon, and it is very excellent to take a walk the last thing at night if one is apt to be sleepless through too great activity of the brain.

Asthma may be speedily relieved by burning in the patient's room saltpetre papers; they are made in the following way: Soak blotting-paper in a solution of strong saltpetre in water. Dry before the fire or in a slow oven. Cut the paper in strips, and burn one when necessary. They should be kept in a dry place.

Girls who suffer from Pimples find that watercress is an excellent blood-purifier, and it should be eaten daily with breakfast; it should, however, be very carefully washed before it is eaten.

An Early Morning Drink. Those who suffer from heaviness in the morning, or indigestion, *&c.,* should drink, on rising, the juice of half a lemon in a teacupful of cold water. This cleans the palate and stimulates the secretion of the gastric juices.

FACSIMILE OF BOTTLE.

For a Severe Cold in the Head. A simple plan of treatment is to plug the nostrils with cotton-wool, which has been dipped in glycerine. This relieves the irritation and congestion so distressing in this ailment.

Nervousness. Distinguished by the liability of the sufferer to start and become discomposed by any sudden noise, or the appearance of anyone when not expected, and chiefly due to general weakness. In such cases the system should be strengthened by means of nourishing food, bathing, outdoor exercise, and a course of quinine wine until the symptoms have disappeared.

Mutton Suet is such an excellent household remedy that no one should be without it. Procure a little from the butcher, render it down, run into cakes, and keep it in use. It is an excellent remedy for dry lips and chapped hands, to which it should be applied every night. For cuts and bruises it is almost indispensable. For a sore it should be applied spread on a linen rag. If the suet becomes hard by keeping it can easily be melted when required.

To Prepare Beef Juice for infants and invalids who are ill, take lean rump steak, cut it into thick pieces, place it over a hot coal fire for a moment to warm, and then squeeze it in a lemon squeezer, which should have been previously warmed by dipping in warm water. Let the juice flow out into a glass, and then season it with a little salt. A teaspoonful may be given every two hours to infants under one year, and a tablespoonful to children over five, or to adults.

For Feverish Patients, Apple Tea is a most useful beverage. Take four large cooking apples, cut them in quarters with the peel on. Cut a lemon into thin slices, leaving the rind on, sprinkle over the whole six ounces of crushed loaf sugar. Place in a jug and over it pour two quarts of boiling water, cover until cold, and it will be fit to drink.

Fruit as a Restorative. Fruit-eating is a restorative of the system. Peaches, plums, and apples, especially the latter, are good for brain-workers and those of sedentary habits. The fruits must be eaten in their natural state, without milk, sugar, or cream. If too acid, a piece of bread will correct that. Nothing will improve the complexion so much as eating good sound fruit. Don't eat it at night-time, that is the only thing to observe.

An Orange eaten the first thing in the morning will cure dyspepsia sooner than anything else.

Apples are excellent in many cases of illness, and are far better than salts, oils, and pills. Every man of sedentary habits, and whose liver is sluggish, should eat an apple daily.

Cold Feet. The following simple remedy for cold feet has been found to be very successful: When retiring at night have in your room two small baths. Fill one with quite cold water and the other with water as hot as you can bear it. Soak your feet in the hot water, and on taking them out plunge them immediately into the cold. Repeat this several times, finishing with the cold, and dry thoroughly with a rough towel.

The Best Time to Administer Laudanum. *A fit of hysterics* may be prevented by the administration of thirty drops of laudanum, and as many of ether. When it has taken place open the windows, sprinkle cold water on the face, and *give the patient a glass of wine*. Avoid excitement, and tight lacing.

A Useful Remedy for Chapped Lips. Take three teaspoonfuls of quince seeds, add to half a pint of water, boil down to a quarter of a pint, then add two ounces of glycerine, and scent with two or three drops of oil of roses. This preparation is also useful for chapped hands.

A Cold in the Head is one of the most disagreeable of troubles. Here is a snuff which is valuable in allaying the annoyance: Menthol, six grains; powdered boracic acid, two drachms; subnitrate of bismuth and powdered benzoin, of each three drachms. A pinch of this may be used five or six times daily.

HINTS TOWARDS FIRST AID

Insects in the Ear should be removed by gently syringing with warm water.

When any one Faints he or she should be laid at once on the floor, *as flat as possible*, as this tends to restore equilibrium of circulation. In this, as in all else, Nature seems to have been provided with her own remedy, for, if permitted, the victim of a fainting-fit would fall prone of her own accord.

A Sprained Ankle should be put at once into hot water for ten minutes. If the pain is severe put a bran bag dipped into hot vinegar on to it.

Bleeding. Hot water—which must be really hot, and not tepid merely—is a valuable remedy in cases of bleeding. Bleeding from the stomach may be controlled by making the patient sip hot water, and nose-bleeding may also be stopped by making the patient sit *with the feet in very hot water*.

Violent Shocks will sometimes stun a person, and he will remain unconscious. Loosen anything that is tight, apply smelling-salts to the nose, and hot bottles to the feet.

WHAT TO DO WHEN PEOPLE CHOKE.

- The substance which causes the choking may either be at the top of the throat, at the entrance to the gullet, or lower down. If at the upper part of the throat, prompt action will often remove it, either by thrusting the finger and thumb into the mouth and pulling the obstruction away. If it cannot be reached so as to pull it away, *a piece of whalebone, a quill, or even a pen holder*— anything at hand—should be seized and pushed down as a probe, so as to force the substance down the gullet.

- Tickling the back of the mouth with a feather so as to produce sudden retching will sometimes dislodge it; a sharp blow on the back will perhaps displace it, or *a sudden splashing of cold water on the face*, which causes involuntary gasping. Should the patient become insensible, it *must not be assumed that he is dead*; on the contrary, cases have often been quoted when the best results have followed on the person having been placed in a recumbent position, the piece of food being extracted, and animation restored by means of the same treatment resorted to in the case of insensibility from immersion in water.

- *Blowing Forcibly into the Ear* gives great assistance in coughing up anything which a person has imperfectly swallowed, and which threatens to choke him.
- *Raw Egg swallowed immediately* will be generally found to carry down a fish bone that cannot be got up from the throat.

POISONS AND THEIR ANTIDOTES

Arsenic. Its Antidote.—Lime water in copious draughts; emetic of mustard or sulphate of zinc, flaxseed tea, infusion of slippery elm, white of egg; hydrated oxide of iron or dialysed iron; milk, and equal parts of lime water and linseed oil.

Belladonna Tincture. Its Antidote —Emetic of mustard, or of ten grains of sulphate of copper.

Chloroform. Its Antidote.—Fresh, pure air and artificial respiration. Hold the patient up by the heels.

Opium. Its Antidote.—Strong emetic of mustard or other safe emetic, with stomach-pump; dash cold water in the face; keep awake and in motion; strong coffee and artificial respiration.

Phosphorus. Its Antidote.—Emetic of mustard or other safe emetic, crude spirits of turpentine; sulphate of copper should be given in diluted solution, three grains every five minutes until vomiting is induced.

Prussic Acid (contained in oil of almonds, fruit kernels, &c.). Its Antidote.—Carbonate of potash, followed by mixed sulphates of iron. Emetics.

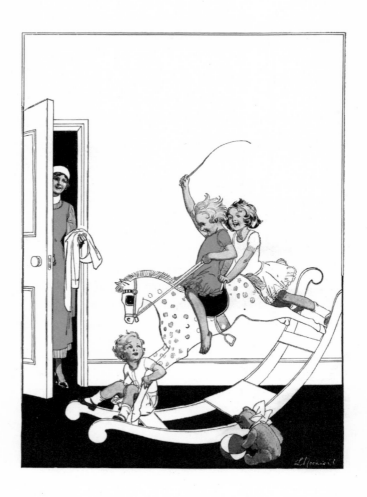

CHAPTER THREE

In the Nursery

BRINGING UP BABY

To Keep Babies Covered at Night. A good plan is to sew a large button on the coverlet, and attach a long white tape with a loop to each corner of the bedstead. After the child is tucked in, fasten the tapes on the bedstead to the buttons on the top coverlet. This keeps the other things from getting moved and the child cannot pull or kick the clothes off him.

A FIRST FOOD FOR INFANTS.

Boiled cow's milk	1 teacupful.
Boiling water	1 teacupful
Thin barley-water	½ teacupful
Cream	1 dessert spoonful
Sugar of Milk	1 teaspoonful.

This makes an excellent food for infants deprived of their natural nourishment, up to the age of four or five months.

RULES ON THE TREATMENT OF CHILDREN.

- Never pamper children, or reward them with eatables.
- Always take care that the child's food is well cooked. Give no new bread.
- Avoid seasoned dishes, fried and salted meats, pastry, uncooked vegetables and unripe fruit, wine, and rich cakes.
- Vary the food from day to day, but avoid variety at one meal.
- Never tempt the appetite when disinclined for food.
- Insist on all children thoroughly masticating and chewing their food.
- Never *plait the hair* of children under eleven or twelve years of age.
- Give all sweets and confectionery in a sparing manner.
- Begin early to form habits of personal cleanliness and delicacy.
- Dress small children in flannel, especially at night. Flannel combinations are better than night-dresses.
- Attend to the size and form of all children's shoes, so that their feet shall not be cramped.
- Avoid keeping the child's head too warm or its feet too cold.

Never Use Baby-Talk to a child learning to speak, as this retards its acquiring distinct speech.

Every Woman ought to be able to sing, if only that she may be able to sing a child to sleep. There is nothing more soothing to a wakeful baby than the lullaby, and this is pretty well proved by its universal popularity amongst all nations. There is no better way of inducing a child to sleep than by gently rubbing its hand or face one way, singing at the same time some low, monotonous song.

If a Child is afraid of his Bath it is a good plan to put a sheet over the bath so as to conceal the water, and placing the child on the sheet, lower it gently into the water.

How to Lift a Child. In lifting a child both hands should be used, and so placed as to lift the body about the waist, or hips, the body being thus raised without any force being exerted upon the arms. *The arms of a child were*

never intended to serve as handles for the purpose of lifting or carrying. Strains, dislocations, and fractures causing deformity and imperfect use of arm or shoulder, or both, result from such careless handling of the arms of a child, which were designed only for the child's use in doing things within its strength.

It is Extremely Improper to consider every noise of an infant as a claim upon our assistance, and to intrude either food or drink, with a view to satisfy its supposed wants.

How Long a Child Should Sleep. A healthy baby for the first two months or so spends most of its time asleep. After that a baby should have at least two hours' sleep in the forenoon and one hour in the afternoon, and it is quite possible to teach almost any infant to adopt this as a regular

habit. Even to the age of four or five years a child should have one hour of sleep, or at least rest in bed, before its dinner, and it should be put to bed at six or seven in the evening, and left undisturbed for twelve or fourteen hours.

During growth there must be ample sleep if the brain is to develop to its full extent, and the more nervous, excitable, or precocious a child is, the longer sleep should it get if its intellectual progress is not to come to a premature standstill, or its life be cut short at an early age. Up to the fifteenth year most young people require ten hours, and till the twentieth year nine hours. After that every one finds out how much he or she requires, though as a general rule six or eight hours are necessary. Eight hours' sleep will prevent more *nervous derangements* in women than any medicine can cure.

Knee-Caps. When little children crawl about they are apt
to wear out the knees of their stockings very much, and it is
a good plan to let them have knee-caps for crawling. They
can be made as follows: Cut from soft black leather a circular
piece three inches in diameter. Make a straight cut of three-
quarters of an inch in each of the four opposite sides, and
overlay these cut edges one half-inch, and sew flat. Tack them
with a few firm stitches to the stocking. If they are the same
colour as the stocking they are not unsightly, and they are an
immense saving from continual darning.

The Girls. When there are girls at home, it is an excellent plan to allow each one in turn to assume the responsibility of housekeeping for a certain time. It is good for girls to be made to take a measure of responsibility concerning household tasks. Let them, in succession, have for a week at a time charge of the bedrooms, the mending, the cooking, and even the buying for the family – all of course under proper supervision – and their faculties of reason, perception, judgement, and discrimination will be more developed in one month of such training than in six months of common schooling.

Surveillance. The greatest art in educating children consists in a continued vigilance over all their actions, without ever giving them an opportunity of discovering that they are guided and watched.

If you wish to Cultivate a Gossiping, Meddling Spirit in your children, be sure when they come home from church, a visit, or any other place where you do not accompany them, to ply them with questions concerning what everybody wore, and what everybody said and did. This will be a vehicle of mischief which will only serve to narrow them.

As They Get Older. Allowance must be made for the difficult periods which occur; the coming of adolescence, for example, develops *odd traits of character* which are, if wisely treated, but temporary.

HOW TO RAISE A HEALTHY CHILD

Nervous Children should never be scolded or ridiculed. They suffer quite enough without threats or sarcasm. Their awkwardness in company, or their grimaces when alone, are not to be noticed; grimaces or twitching of the hands and muscles so often seen in children of a highly nervous temperament are danger-signals, as they are frequently only the beginning of St. Vitus' dance, a serious disease of the nerves. No mention should be made to the child of such antics, but it is well if they appear that a doctor should be consulted, and the little one thoroughly examined.

Children should never be allowed to drink water when they are heated, as dangerous internal chills may result from this.

Hot Milk is a good medium in which to give children castor oil. Take a large wine glass, fill one-third with hot milk, put in the castor oil, then pour over it enough milk to fill the glass. If the child can be induced to drink the whole without stopping, the taste of the oil will not be detected.

Flatulence. Children brought up by hand are very subject to flatulency and should often have a little caraway seed mixed with their food. Fennel-water is another excellent remedy. The dose is a teaspoonful for infants, and from one to four teaspoonfuls for adults. In order to make fennel-water a pound of bruised seeds is added to two gallons of water, and one is distilled off.

Squinting in adult life is often due to the placing of the cradle where it receives a bad or false light. The baby on awaking is forced to squint. A child's bed should therefore be placed with discernment.

If a Child be Thin or inclined to rickets he may have a little bread dipped in bacon fat, although it should not be given to children as a rule, as it is indigestible and apt to spoil the complexion.

A Mustard Bath is much superior to the simple warm bath for bringing out the rash in eruptive fevers, and is a powerful stimulant when the child is failing rapidly from any cause. It is prepared by adding from one to two heaped tablespoonfuls of mustard to one gallon of water.

Children's Teeth should be carefully examined by a dentist before they are taken away for their holidays, and this is especially important for those who go to school. The slightest speck of decay ought to be removed before it spreads.

To Prevent Constipation, the following to be taken after the bath every morning is very useful: Sift some of the finest Scotch oatmeal through coarse muslin, and of the flour thus obtained blend a teaspoonful with a little cold milk; add a little salt, and pour over it a teacupful of boiling milk.

Delicate Children are often made much more so by being kept in hot rooms, and not allowed to have proper ventilation. The coddled child very seldom develops into a hardy man or woman, and as many of the ailments of middle and old age can be traced to the careless ignorance of those in charge of children.

Currants should never be given to little children, as they are difficult to digest and are apt to cause diarrhoea.

Giving Castor Oil to Children is often a serious proceeding in view of the fuss the little ones will make over the dose. A French plan, which seems excellent, is to put the oil into a pan over the fire, and to break an egg into it, stirring the mixture up. Flavoured with a little salt, the valuable but disagreeable-tasting oil can be swallowed with ease and comfort to all concerned.

Crooked legs. The moment you perceive that a child's legs are inclined to be crooked, take care not to allow him to walk. *Leave him to himself on the carpet*, where he can roll about as he likes, and the little legs will soon get straight again.

Cheap Toys. A great deal of amusement is afforded, when the children are allowed at table, by dolls made by running a stick through a shiny mandarin orange, and thrusting it into the neck of a wine-bottle; then a face is "nicked" out from the peel of the orange, more or less saucy according to the humour of the maker. From a piece of brown paper a cloak and hood are improvised, and behold a yellow-faced little bottle-bodied woman.

HANDICRAFTS FOR LITTLE FOLK

FUN TO BE HAD WITH EMPTY SPOOLS

Blowing Bubbles

Mix strong soap-suds, dip one end of a large spool in the water, wet the spool, then blow. These wooden blowers last a long time, with no danger of breaking when accidentally dropped on the floor.

With a Ball

Take an empty spool and stick a common wire hairpin partially into the hole, bend the hairpin slightly down against the edges of the hole, do the same with three more hairpins, and you will have a spool with a funnel-like opening of hairpins at the top. In the funnel place a small, light-weight ball made of a crushed bit of paper wound around with thread. Raise the spool to your lips and blow gently. The ball will rise and fall in mid-air.

HOMEMADE ANIMALS
The Envelope Frog

Draw the outlines of your frog on the envelope as shown here, then cut along the lines you have drawn. The under part of the body follows the edge of the lower lap of the envelope from front to hind leg. Now flatten out the fold at the top and bend the paper under at the corners, which forms the head and tail. Cut a slit along the folded edge of the head for the mouth, pull the lower part down and the mouth will open wide as a frog's naturally does. By working the lower jaw the flog can be made to snap at imaginary flies. Draw the eyes as shown and bend down the lower part of the body along the dotted line, spread out the hind legs, and Master Frog is finished.

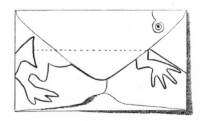

The Clothespin Rooster

You can make cunning, downy roosters simply of raw cotton and clothespins. Slide the prongs of two clothespins into each other. Be sure the clothespins, when together, stand firm on the prong ends, for these form the legs and feet. With a string tie a piece of raw cotton over the head of one clothespin, and tie it again around the bottom.

Use your fingers to shape the top cotton into the form of a head; gently pull a little out to make the beak, and twist it into a point. Lay the centre of a generous piece of cotton over the head of the second clothespin, plait the loose ends, and fasten with a string. Cut the folded end rounded on top, and slit it up a short distance into a wide fringe, to form the long feathers of the rooster's tail.

With another piece of cotton cover the back and sides of the rooster, as you would a saddle on a horse, and stick with paste. Then, with the top of a wire hairpin, push the edges of the cover, front and back, in between the open prongs of the clothespin. Ink round bits of paper and paste on his face for eyes; make his comb of red tissue paper, and you will have a fine rooster which can actually move his little cotton head up and down as you wish.

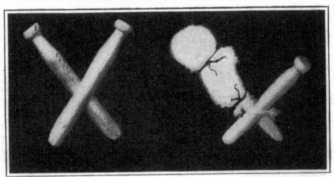

CHAPTER
FOUR

In the
Kitchen

COOKERY is an art upon which so much of our daily comfort and health depends, that it is of the highest importance that it be well done. A good housewife suffers nothing to be lost or spoiled. Scraps are put to proper use, and may be brought to table in a new and attractive guise.

THE ART OF AFTERNOON TEA

When making tea be sure that the water is freshly boiled. Water that has been boiling for some time has a very flat taste, and even the most expensive and best-flavoured tea will have anything but a pleasant taste unless made with water that is just boiling.

To avoid the usual flat taste of boiled water, it should be poured from jug to jug in order to let the air pass through it.

Use soft water where possible, for it softens and opens the tea-leaves more thoroughly than hard water.

Tea Made with Boiling Milk instead of water, and allowed to stand for four minutes before being poured out, is excellent, and very nourishing.

To render Milk more Digestible, when it is apt to disagree with one, shake it thoroughly for five minutes.

THE CONTINENTAL TEA BASKET

A Cause of Indigestion. The Drinking of tea which has stood for a long time on the hob is one of the chief causes of indigestion among working women. In order to make tea of the best kind, water which has boiled up for the first time should be poured over the leaves and allowed to stand for not more than five minutes. It should be then poured into a second teapot, which may be kept hot if desired.

Other indelicate effects. Tea should never be drunk immediately after dinner, or after a heavy meal, as if so taken it is apt to cause *flatulence and other digestive troubles*. A tea-dinner or tea with meat is not wholesome, and upsets people who have weak digestions, and the drinking of strong tea causes sleeplessness, shaking of the hands and other nervous afflictions.

The use of cream. It is well to know that, to be as free as possible from injurious qualities, the cream should not be poured into the cup until *after the tea*, as the scalding tea poured into the cream causes the tannin to form a leathery compound, which is very indigestible. Contrariwise, the cream should always be put into the cups before pouring out coffee.

To Toast and Butter Muffins. Very few persons know how to toast and butter muffins *properly*. As a rule they are either half-toasted or burnt and not buttered well. Having a clear fire, toast it a nice brown, not hurrying the business. Then tear the muffin apart with two forks, lay a lump of butter in the centre, put on the top, and divide in wedge-like sections. Muffins so treated are not the indigestible edibles so often offered, and refused by all such as are wise, unless they happen to possess the gastric power ascribed to the ostrich.

CLEANLINESS IS NEXT TO GODLINESS

To Clean a Knife that has been used for Cutting Onions, hold it under the cold water tap. It is a mistake to use hot water to remove the smell of onions from a knife.

Provide one knife labelled 'Onions', which can be readily bought, thereby saving yourself from the terrible taste of *onion-flavoured bread-and-butter*.

The Problem with Cabbage. Sometimes the most careful washing will not remove the flavour and odour of food from the utensil in which it was cooked. This is frequently the case with fish, onions, cabbage, &c., but there is a remedy which may be a little trouble, and yet it is well worth trying. After any of these articles have been cooked, wash the utensil well with soap and water. Then nearly fill it with cold water, and for each quart of water add about a tablespoonful of dissolved washing soda. Place on the fire, and let the water get boiling hot. Now turn the water into the sink. Rinse the utensil with clean water, and on wiping it dry it will be found perfectly sweet.

To Purify Saucepans. A Saucepan in which rice, oats, or anything sticky has been cooked, may be very easily cleaned by putting in *a cupful of ashes* when you take it off the fire, and then filling with water.

A Good Egg-beater may be spoiled by ill-treatment. If washed in hot soap and water, which takes the oil out, it will not work well. To keep in good order wash it by holding it under the cold water tap. This will remove egg, dough, or cream better than hot water.

Glasses used for Milk should be thoroughly rinsed in cold water before they are washed. Hot water drives the milk into the glass.

78

Tablecloths ought to be slightly starched; this will make them last clean and retain their fresh appearance for a much longer time.

Frying-Pans should be cleaned by being rubbed with salt the minute they are done with, and wiped clean with a cloth.

Pudding and Pie Dishes, cups and saucers, after being used for baking purposes, are frequently marked with brown stains, which are sometimes difficult to remove. This may be managed, however, by means of powdered whiting (powdered calcium carbonate), which, applied on a damp flannel, will speedily take off the marks.

Old Pots and Kettles that have become stained, or have a lingering odour, may be immersed in cold soapsuds and boiled, when they will come out as good as new.

If Milk be Filtered through Cotton its germs are largely intercepted, while no cream is lost. Cotton-wool is well known to be an effective germ filter, and a pad of cotton-wool placed over the mouth enables a person to breathe easily amid fire and smoke, because it prevents the irritating particles from entering the lungs.

Do not let Knives be dropped into hot dish-water. It is a good plan to have a large tin pot to wash them in, just high enough to wash the blades without wetting the handles.

Knives are often ruined by pressing too hard on the knife-board when cleaning them, in the effort to get out stains. This may be done more rapidly, and without fear of spoiling them, by simply rubbing them up and down a few times with a damp cork dipped in emery powder. When the stains have gone the knives may be polished on the board; but it can be dispensed with altogether, if preferred.

CORRECT COOKING TECHNIQUES

The Temperature of an Oven may be easily reduced while cooking by placing a bowl of water in it.

Warm Dishes for the Table by immersing them in hot water, not by standing them in the oven.

Frying the crucial test. To be successful with this almost crucial test of a cook's powers, the fat must be absolutely boiling; this condition is only arrived at when the fat leaves off spluttering and becomes still. When perfectly boiling, fish, meat, or sweets may be in the same fat without transmitting their different flavours.

When Fat in a frying-pan becomes hot before you can use it, put in a dry crust of bread, it will not burn so long as it has something to do, only when it is left idle.

When the Fat is on the Fire it is never wise to throw water upon it. If fat in a pan boils over, and there are ashes convenient to throw on the blaze, it is the surest and safest way to put it out.

Fish are Scaled and fowls plucked more quickly if dipped into boiling water for an instant.

In Roasting Meat turn with a spoon instead of a fork, as the latter pierces the meat and lets the juices escape.

When Saucepans Boil Over and cause an unpleasant smell, *sprinkle some cedar wood dust* on the stove, and a pleasant odour will succeed the disagreeable one. Cedar wood dust is a great boon to the housewife, and as it is only the waste of the pencil manufacturer it is very inexpensive.

Icing for Cake may be prevented from cracking, when cut, by adding one tablespoonful of sweet cream to each unbeaten egg.

Gravy from Pies may be preventing from running over, by thrusting little funnels of white paper into the cuts on the top, through which the steam may escape and the gravy boil up, and then run back into the pie again when it stops cooking.

 GARNISHES

- *Parsley* is the most universal garnish for all kinds of poultry, fish, butter, cheese, and so forth.
- *Horseradish* is the garnish for roast beef, and for fish in general; for the latter, slices of lemon are sometimes laid alternately with the horseradish.
- *Slices of lemon* for boiled fowl, turkey, and fish, and for roast veal and calf's head.
- *Carrot* in slices for boiled beef, hot or cold.
- *Barberries*, fresh or preserved, for game.
- *Red beetroot* sliced for cold meat, boiled beef, and salt fish.
- *Fried smelts* as garnish for turbot.
- *Fried sausages* or force-meat balls are placed round turkey, capon, or fowl.
- *Lobster coral* and parsley round boiled fish.
- *Fennel* for mackerel and salmon, either fresh or pickled.
- *Currant jelly* for game, also for custard or bread pudding.
- *Seville orange* or lemon in slices for wild ducks, pigeons, teal, &c.
- *Mint*, either with or without parsley, for roast lamb, either hot or cold.
- *Pickled gherkins*, capers, or onions, for some kinds of boiled meat and stews.

 ALL ABOUT EGGS

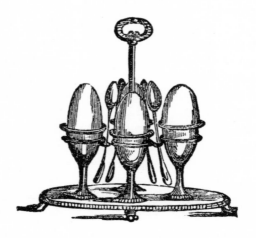

An accompaniment to coffee. Women who are obliged to make an early morning start may find the following hint profitable: "When I am going to town for a day's shopping," a lady says, "nine times out of ten I have to go without my breakfast, or snatch it in great haste. I do not mind now since I have learned how to condense it. *I break an egg into my coffee-cup*, and fill it with clear, scalding coffee. As soon as it is cool I swallow it, and am at once nourished and stimulated for hours."

A Simple Way of Testing Eggs. If the end of a fresh egg is applied to the tongue it feels cold; that of a stale egg feels warm. This is due to the white of a fresh egg being in contact with the shell, and abstracting the heat from the tongue more rapidly than does the air-bubble in the stale one. Fresh eggs are more transparent in the centre, stale ones at the end.

Hints about Eggs. Boiled eggs which adhere to the shell are fresh. A good egg will sink in water. Stale eggs are glassy and smooth of shell. The shell of a fresh egg has a lime-like surface. A boiled egg which is dull and dries quickly on the shell when taken from the kettle, is fresh. Eggs which have been packed in lime look stained, and show the action of the lime on the surface. If packed in bran for a long time, eggs acquire a musty smell.

The age of eggs. Eggs directly from the nest are said to be less rich and appetising than when a day or two old. For invalids, day-old eggs are recommended *as just the thing*.

New Egg Dish. When you are tired of plain boiled or fried eggs try this way of serving them for breakfast: butter a pie-dish and cover the bottom with breadcrumbs; then break enough eggs for your party, and drop them on the dish, and cover with a layer of breadcrumbs; sprinkle pepper and salt all over this, and put some little lumps of butter on it. Bake in a quick oven for five minutes.

Eggs when Boiling, Frequently Burst. This is caused by their being too full of air, and may be prevented by pricking one end with a needle before putting them into the water. This makes an outlet for the air, and avoids any possibility of their bursting.

To Boil Eggs for Invalids. Bring the water to the boil, then take the saucepan off the fire and place the egg in it for five minutes. This will cook the egg perfectly without making the white hard and indigestible. It is also well to boil an egg intended for a young child in this manner.

When beating up the Whites of Eggs add a tiny pinch of salt, because this will cut them up and make them frothy much quicker, as well as making the froth stiffer than it otherwise would be.

FISH, FLESH AND FOWL

When Boiling Salmon the water should always be brought to the boil, but for all other fish the water should only be warm.

Fish is not to be depended upon to *develop the brain*, as is commonly supposed. The phosphorus contained in it has its value, but nothing is so good for brain development as exercise and hard work, and thinking out difficult problems.

To Remove the Muddy Taste of fresh water fish place them in cold water well salted for several hours before cooking.

The Importance of Juice. Roast Joints that should be Juicy come to the table as dry as a board, because the oven was not hot enough at first to instantly harden the outer surface of the meat and prevent the escape of its juice. Meat should never be kept on Ice, for this absorbs the juice. It should be kept in a cool place free from damp.

Mint Sauce renders lamb, with which it is eaten, more easy of digestion.

Potted Meat. Take any well-roasted or boiled meat, remove all gristle, hard pieces, and fat from it, mince, and then pound it in a mortar, with a little butter, reduced gravy, and a spoonful of Worcestershire sauce, beat it to a smooth paste, seasoning during the process with pounded cloves and allspice, mace, or grated nutmeg, salt, and a little cayenne. Put the mixture into pots, press it closely down, cover with clarified butter, and keep it in a cool, dry place.

Plucking. The size of a young Fowl may be known before plucking by the largeness of the feet and leg-joints. After plucking, a thin neck and violet thighs may be taken as invariable signs of age and toughness, especially in turkeys and fowls. The age of ducks and geese is tested by their beaks, the lower part of which breaks away quite easily when they are young.

Tough Fowls are rendered as Tender as Chickens by steaming them two hours or so.

To Remove the Strong flavour of poultry, wash the fowl in strong soda water, rinse in cold water, and wipe.

When Cleaning Poultry before cooking it sometimes happens that the gall gets broken by accident. The unpleasant taste thus given to the meat may be removed by soaking it for about half an hour in cold water, to which a handful of soda has been added.

To Make Raw Meat Sandwiches, scrape good juicy meat as fine as possible, put it on a thin slice of bread-and-butter, pepper and salt it, press another slice of bread-and-butter on the top, and cut it into thin strips. These sandwiches should not be prepared until it is time to serve them, for they spoil if allowed to become dry.

FRUIT AND VEGETABLES

THE EFFECTS OF VEGETABLES.

- A pinch of celery seed is a great improvement to pickles, and should be boiled with the other spices in the vinegar.
- Garlic and onions *stimulate the heart* and *help the circulation*; they also promote digestion.
- Tomatoes act on the liver.
- Beetroot is an appetiser, either eaten with vinegar or not.
- Lettuce is cooling, so are currants, yellow plums, and gooseberries.
- Asparagus *clears the blood*, and is most wholesome.
- Mulberries, pears, and strawberries, if quite ripe, are very fattening.
- The most fattening vegetables are carrots, turnips, potatoes, and peas.

Unripe Vegetables. It should always be remembered that unripe and half-grown vegetables are as flavourless and unwholesome as unripe fruit.

Never Warm up a Dish containing Mushrooms is a caution that physicians often give. The process of cooking is in itself proper; but after cooling mushrooms are liable to develop injurious properties, and to become hurtful. Therefore consume freshly cooked mushrooms all at one sitting, and throw away any that may be left over.

Hint: Use a Silver Spoon when Cooking Mushrooms; the silver will be blackened if any injurious property is present.

Nettles. If you gather the young shoots of nettles as soon as they appear – in March or April – and boil the same way as cabbage sprouts, you will find them exceedingly nice and *purifying for the blood*.

The Thick End of the Cucumber. Always begin to cut Cucumbers at the thick end; the thin end often has a bitter taste.

Beetroots should be boiled for one hour in summer, an hour and a half to two hours in winter. Onions of medium size for one hour.

Watercress should always be soaked in brine, rinsed and picked over before being sent to table.

The Leek is a vegetable which should be more widely used than is the case in our households today. It is in all respects a most excellent addition to the bill of fare. It may be safely used by dyspeptics, and is a corrective of *constipation and liver troubles*. It is best eaten stewed, and served with butter or other sauce on toast. It serves to purify the blood, and to keep the skin clear.

To Peel Tomatoes. Cover them with boiling water for half a minute, then lay them in cold water till they are perfectly cold, when the skin can be slipped off quite easily, leaving the tomatoes unbroken, and as firm as before they were scalded.

TIME-TABLE FOR BOILING.

- *Potatoes* half an hour, unless small, when rather less.
- *Peas and asparagus*, twenty to twenty-five minutes.
- *Cabbage and cauliflower*, twenty-five minutes to half an hour.
- *String beans*, if slit or sliced slantwise and thin, twenty-five minutes; if only snapped across, forty minutes.
- *Lima beans*, if very young, half an hour; old, forty to fifty minutes.
- *Carrots and turnips*, forty-five minutes when young; one hour in winter.

Beware of Eating Tinned Fruit at all times, but especially be on your guard against it in the hot weather of summer. Many cases of *cholera* are due, not to the fruit itself, but to its having undergone changes of the nature of decay and putrefaction.

The Danger of a Painted Table. Newly-baked bread should never be placed on a painted table, for it will absorb the smell of the paint.

To Preserve Butter. Boil the butter in a roomy vessel until the scum rises and skim it off as it comes to the surface. When the butter remains in the form of a clear oil-like fluid, carefully pour it off, so as to leave impurities at the bottom. The settlings may be used at once, but the clarified butter will keep.

Hint: Butter put into clean pots and well surrounded with charcoal will keep good for twelve months.

Do not Buy Butter speckled with pinky spots, nor that which has a milky appearance; such butter has not been well washed from the buttermilk, and will quickly turn sour.

Potatoes affected by Frost should be laid in a perfectly dry place for some days after the thaw has commenced. If thawed in daylight they will rot, but if in darkness they do not; nor do they lose much of their natural properties.

Malodorous Flour. Never keep Flour near fish, vegetables, or anything of that kind, for it very easily *absorbs odours*, and may thus be spoilt for cakes or bread-making. Neither should it be kept in a damp place.

Preserve Fish by putting into a jar, covering with good oil, and tying over well to exclude the air.

To Keep Cheese from Moulding or from becoming dry, wrap it in a cloth damp with vinegar, and keep it in a covered dish.

Sour Soup. Bread or Vegetables should never be kept in soup for they will turn it sour.

Eggs become unwholesome if kept in refrigerators; a fungus forms in them which is easily found by the microscope, although it is not noticeable to the taste. This fungus constitutes a danger when we consider how many eggs are consumed by *all classes of society*, and people of delicate constitutions ought to be particularly careful that they eat fresh and not kept eggs.

An Apple kept in the Cake Box will keep moderately rich cake moist for a great length of time, if the apple is renewed when it becomes withered.

If well packed in pulverised charcoal after the usual smoking, ham will keep for years.

To Preserve Cucumbers. When there are more cucumbers in the garden than necessary for daily use, preserve them for the winter. Pare them and slice them, then sprinkle with salt, and leave them for a day. Drain away the brine, and then place the slices of cucumber in a jar with a small quantity of salt between each layer. When the jar is full, tie over with bladder, and put away in a cool place. When required for use soak in fresh water, then serve, with vinegar and oil, in the usual way.

To Protect Fruit. It is very provoking in the depth of winter to find that some of one's choicest fruit has been frostbitten. Many people have advocated the use of newspapers *stitched together to form blankets for the poor*, but not many have remembered that newspapers are a most valuable protection to apples in a store-room into which the frost can penetrate.

Instead of Keeping Parsley in Water, which makes it turn yellow, put it in an air-tight jar in a cool place. This will keep it fresh for some time.

Damp Storage. Various articles of food (amongst others cream cheese) are spoiled if kept in a damp place. Where this is not preventable, a small quantity of dry oats placed around them will keep the air in their immediate vicinity perfectly dry.

Honey should be kept in the dark. The bees, knowing this, work in the dark.

Cans of Milk or Butter can be kept perfectly cold by being wrapped in a cloth and set in a deep dish containing some water where air is circulating. As the cloth absorbs the water, cold is produced by evaporation.

A Larder Hint. Never put away food on tin plates. Fully one-half of the cases of *poison from the use of tinned goods* arise from the articles left over being put back into the tin.

When Tea or Coffee is to be kept, they should never be poured into a tin utensil. Put them into a jug or basin of china or earthenware.

THRIFTY TIPS FOR ECONOMICAL COOKS

Turnip-Peel should always be washed and then added to soups, to which it imparts a delicious flavour.

Save all Cold Vegetables and fry them together with potatoes and plenty of pepper and salt.

Biscuits that have been softened by exposure will become fresh and crisp again by being put into the oven a few minutes.

Cold Meat heated with a little curry powder is far more digestible, and far more nourishing than cold meat alone.

A Cheap Firelighter. The peel of potatoes after being dried in the oven will light the fire quickly instead of using wood, thus saving expense, and being more healthy than if allowed to rot in the dustbin.

To Test the Purity of Coffee pour cold water on it. If the water assumes a brownish hue it may be concluded that there is chicory in it.

Stale Loaves should be *wrapped in a hot cloth* for half a minute, the cloth taken off, and baked in a slow oven for half an hour.

97

A Substitute for Cream. Stir a dessert spoonful of flour into a pint of new milk, taking care that it is perfectly smooth. Simmer it to take off the raw taste of flour. Beat well the yolk of an egg, and stir it gently into the milk. Pass all through a fine sieve.

Hints on Buying Groceries. Buy the best flour, even at extra cost. You can tell it by pressing it tightly in the hand, when it will have a yellowish tinge, and the lines of the skin will be left upon it. Flour and meal of all kinds should be kept in a cool, dry place. When you have found a good flour, buy a year's supply, if you have storing room. In cooking, new flour is not so good as old.

An Oyster-Shell in the tea-kettle will prevent the formation of crust in the inside.

Mustard-Water will cleanse the hands from all odour after peeling onions.

Chopped Onions are a desirable and healthful addition to chicken's food.

A Small Lump of Sugar added to clear soup when boiling up before serving adds brilliancy to its appearance.

A Judicious Blend of different kinds of coffee always produces a better kind than any single type. This mixture ought to be made after roasting, and not before.

The Grounds of Coffee, left after using the liquid, are an excellent ingredient to mix with the earth used in flower-pots. Our grandmothers' custom was to put it on the surface also, in order to keep the earth moist, and they had roses in bloom all the year round in their windows.

Carving and Helping at Table. The carving is not to be done with any appearance of exertion, nor by mere strength in wielding or wrenching the knife; it must be effected with *quietness and neatness*.

 **RECIPES**

GIBLET SOUP

Giblets consist of the head and neck, the feet, the pinions of the wings, the liver, gizzard, and heart. The pinions of the wings, and skin of the neck, require to be scalded, to free them from bits of feather. The beak, which is not used, should be taken from the head, and the skull split. When all the pieces are thoroughly cleaned, put them in 2 pints of stock, and let them boil until they are tender. Take them out, and cut the meat from the bones. Strain the liquor; return it to the saucepan, and thicken with a little kneaded flour and butter. Season with pepper and salt, add the pieces of giblets, and boil for five minutes.

POTATO SALAD

In many houses cold boiled potatoes are considered as waste, and do not make their appearance a second time at table. If cut into slices and dressed with salt, pepper, oil, and vinegar, also, if possible, with beetroot and celery added to them, they compose a most excellent and refreshing salad.

ONION SOUP

is often useful in cases of sleeplessness: Get a large, strong English onion, place it in an earthenware jar, and cover it with coarse brown sugar. Place it in a slow oven, and leave it there for four or five hours or more. Put the resulting syrup into a bottle; a dessert spoonful to be taken on waking in the night.

TO SERVE A TONGUE

If hard, *soak the bullock's tongue in water* all night
before using. Boil it for around three hours. Skin
it before dishing. Garnish with greens or cabbage.

BAKED EGGS

Why should eggs always be boiled when they are so
good baked? Butter a tin or old saucer, and on it
place a raw egg; bake it for about ten minutes, or
till the egg is nicely set. A novel way of baking eggs is
as follows: First prick several holes in the large end
of an egg to allow the escape of the air, as it expands
from the heat; place on a small tin, and bake about
ten minutes.

A WHOLESOME DRINK

A beverage for persons *afflicted with feverish thirst* is made
by pouring two quarts of boiling water over two
teaspoonfuls of pearl barley and two ounces of sugar.
Add the peel of one lemon, let it stand all night, and
strain in the morning.

TOFFEE

Take two pounds of demerara sugar, three-quarters
of a pint of water, four ounces of butter, and a
little lemon-juice. Test it by dropping into cold water,
and when it is done it will be crisp. Before pouring
out into a buttered dish stand the saucepan on the
hob till it is off the boil. Stir the toffee all the time,
and have a good clear fire.

OYSTER PATTIES

Roll puff paste to half an inch in thicknesss, cut in rounds about three inches in diameter, mark the tops with a smaller round, and bake in a brisk oven. Melt butter and flour in a saucepan, and pour on to them the *liquor of two dozen oysters*. Stir until they boil. Beard the oysters, cut them in halves, and add them to the contents of the saucepan, with salt, cayenne pepper, and lemon juice to taste. Add a table-spoon of cream and mix well. Fill the hollows of the patty-cases with the oyster mixture, and put the lids back on again. Serve hot, and garnish with curled parsley.

CAULIFLOWER CUTLETS

Wash a cauliflower well in salted water, and boil. When nearly done take it out and drain thoroughly. Put into a dish with salt, pepper, and vinegar, heat this over the fire. Make a batter of three tablespoonfuls of flour, two eggs, salt, a little oil, and a teaspoonful of brandy. Make this into a thin paste. Dip each piece of cauliflower into the batter, and fry to a light brown. Serve very hot with a squeeze of lemon.

POTATO ROLLS

Mash some boiled potatoes. To three teacupfuls of potato add half a teacupful of butter, two eggs beaten up until stiff, two tablespoonfuls of baking-powder, one half-teacupful of milk, a half-teaspoonful of pepper, and a little salt. Beat together and bake in rolls.

TO MAKE DELICIOUS RUSKS

However careful one is to prevent waste of bread, it
is impossible in a household to have no spare pieces.
Everyone uses these up in different ways—sometimes in
puddings, sometimes as breadcrumbs, *&c*. Here is a very
popular receipt: Break the crusts into pieces about the
size of a large walnut, dip them for a moment into milk in
which has been mixed a little salt and a pinch of cayenne
pepper. Place the pieces on a baking-sheet, and bake in a
moderate oven until they assume a golden colour. When
cold, store the rusks in a tin.

GRUEL

Put 2 table-spoonfuls of groats and 1 pint of water into a
saucepan, and let them boil for at least one hour. Add 1
gill of milk, and strain through a hair-sieve. Season with
butter and sugar, and serve hot.

A CHEAP SAVOURY ENTRÉE

Put a piece of butter the size of a walnut into a saucepan,
slice a Spanish onion into it, and let it simmer for five
minutes; then cut a quarter of a pound of cheese into
small pieces and put it in; pour in half a cupful of sweet
milk, and stir well till all is melted; add a little salt, beat
up one egg and pour it into the saucepan, stir well for two
minutes, then serve.

BROWNING FOR SOUPS

Take four ounces of moist sugar and put it into a frying-
pan; set it over a clear fire, and when the sugar is melted

it will be frothy. Remove it a little from the fire until it becomes brown; keep stirring all the time. Add claret until the pan is nearly full, but take care that it does not boil over. Then add salt and lemon-peel, a few cloves, and a little mace; boil gently for five or ten minutes. When cold put it carefully into a bottle. It will then be ready for use.

OYSTER KETCHUP

Take some fresh oysters. Wash them in their own liquor, strain it, pound them in a marble mortar. To a pint of oysters pour *a pint of sherry*; boil them up, and add an ounce of salt, two drachms of pounded mace, and one of cayenne. Let it just boil up again, skim it, and rub it through a sieve. When cold, bottle it, cork well, and seal it down.

EGGS AND CREAM

Whip an egg for fifteen minutes, then whip in one and a half tablespoonfuls of cream and, by degrees, a large dessert spoonful of brandy. Use directly it is mixed; a little sugar may be added if desired.

TOAST WATER

Take the upper crust of a stale loaf, about an inch and a half thick. Toast it very brown and dry before the fire, but do not burn it. Place it in a jug containing 1 quart of cold water. Cover for one hour, strain through muslin, and serve. Toast water should be made fresh every day.

POTTED FISH

Cut fresh herrings or mackerel in thick pieces, pack them
in a stone jar with plenty of peppercorns, a blade of mace,
a shallot, pinch of salt, bay leaf, and a gill of vinegar. Tie
the lid down and let them soak several hours in a very slow
oven, or, better still, leave them in a baker's oven all night.

LEMONADE WITHOUT LEMONS

This is a very good kind to make for bottling and will last
some time. Two or three teaspoonfuls added to a tumbler of
cold water makes a refreshing substitute for lemon squash.
Take five pounds of loaf sugar and one quart of cold water
and let it boil gradually. When quite boiling pour it on
to three ounces of citric acid and two drams of essence of
lemon. When this is quite cold, bottle for use. The cost is
small, and all the ingredients very easy to procure.

CELERY SOUP

Wash six good heads of celery thoroughly in salt and water.
Peel two onions and cut them up small with the celery. Stew
for some hours in the stock with one ounce of pearl barley
and a small bunch of herbs. Before serving, season the soup
with pepper and salt, and remove the herbs.

MOSS BLANCMANGE

There is a moss found on the seashores of Iceland which,
when boiled in milk, forms a nice smooth white jelly.
Iceland Moss is sold by druggists and grocers, and resembles
dry seaweed of a yellowish colour. Pick all gritty or sandy

particles from the moss, soak in water for twelve hours, and drain. Place in a saucepan on the fire with a pint of milk. When the moss is dissolved, leaving nothing but a few thready fibres, strain it into a mould. When cold, it will have all the appearance of a firm blancmange.

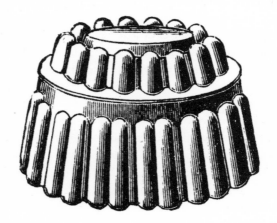

TO BOIL CALF'S HEAD

Clean and split the head, and take out the brains. Lay the head in cold water for two hours, to whiten it. Then tie it in a cloth, and boil for two and a half hours. *Boils the brains in vinegar* and water for twenty minutes. Put one half of the brains into the sauce. Skin the tongue; put the remainder of the brains round it in a separate dish, and serve at the same time with the head. Pour the sauce over the head, and serve very hot. *Sauce.*– Melt butter in a small pan. Add flour, and when well mixed, pour on the liquor from the head; stir until boiling. Season and *add the parsley and brains.*

SHEEP'S-HEAD PIE

After a sheep's head and trotters have been properly cleaned, simmer slowly for five or six hours. Whilst warm, remove the bones, and cut the head and feet neatly into small pieces. Have ready some bacon and oysters or hard-boiled eggs sliced. Place *a layer of sheep's head* in the bottom of the pie-dish. Sprinkle over it a mixture of pepper, salt, mace, and ginger; then put a layer of bacon and eggs. Repeat till the dish is filled. Add a cupful of the liquor in which the head was cooked. Cover with pastry; bake and hour and a half.

EEL PIE

Skin two eels; cut off their heads, tails and fins, and clean them. Cut them in pieces, and lay them in the pie-dish, seasoning with pepper and salt. Make a gravy to pour over them, by boiling the heads, tails, and fins in the water, pepper and salt for half an hour. Strain, and when cool thicken with flour, and pour it on the eels. Cover, and bake for about an hour.

CHAPTER
FIVE

Happy
Housekeeping

MAKING DO & MENDING

Home Dressmakers who have difficulty in pressing curved seams will find a common kitchen rolling-pin a very good pressing-board, if a piece of paper be wrapped round it.

Limp Veils can be stiffened by dipping them in cold water, then pulling them out straight and hanging them up to dry.

Woollen Stockings, when too old for wear, are exceedingly useful for cleaning purposes. The tops should be cut off and sewn together until sufficiently thick. Remnants of flannel and woollen materials may be utilised in the same way, and make very good interlinings for iron and kettle-holders.

To Restore Faded Cashmere sponge with equal parts of *alcohol and ammonia*, diluted with a little warm water.

Do not wear the same Stockings on two successive days, but keep two pairs for wearing alternately, hanging each to dry and air when not in use. Every night bathe the feet in tepid water, and rub hard with a coarse towel.

Old Furs when too shabby to wear may be made into foot-warmers, and will give comfort to those whose work keeps them away from the fire. Join the fur like a bag (wool or hair facing), tack it firmly on to the footstool or hassock, and cover with a piece of tapestry or cretonne; the feet are kept perfectly warm between the fur.

Beads and Amber Ornaments often look dirty and their owners hardly know what to do with them to restore their polished appearance. The best way is to rub the amber with a little whiting made damp first, following this by the application of some olive oil, afterwards rubbing dry and well polishing with a piece of flannel.

Brush Dark Dresses thoroughly with a clean, hard brush dipped in blue water, and then hang them up to dry. This revives dark blue and black materials, and makes them look almost as good as new.

Do not throw away old Kid Gloves. Cut off the hands, and save the arms of your long, soiled evening gloves. Use them for polishing silver, mirrors, cut glass, and jewels. Sew two of the long pieces into irregularly-shaped bags for carrying the pieces of a silver toilet set when travelling. It preserves the silver from scratching and tarnishing. Out of old tan or grey gloves you can make charming bags for carrying your opera-glasses in. Cut the kid in the same pattern as is used for these silk and velvet bags, line it with China silk, and trace in pen and water colours, or silk, your initials on the outside.

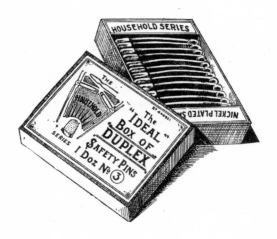

HINTS ON DYEING FABRIC

To those who wish to have certain fabrics dyed, the following information may be found useful as regards the colours they will take:

- *Black material* can only be dyed black, brown, dark green, dark crimson, dark claret, dark olive.
- *Brown* can only be dyed black, dark green, dark brown, dark claret, dark olive.
- *Dark Green.* – Black, dark brown, dark green, dark claret, dark crimson, dark olive.
- *Light Green.* – Dark green, black, dark brown, dark crimson, dark claret, dark olive.
- *Dark Crimson.* – Black, brown, dark crimson, dark claret.
- *Light Crimson* will take the same colours as dark crimson.
- *Claret.* – Black, brown, dark crimson, dark claret.
- *Fawn* will take dark crimson, dark green, black, brown, dark claret.
- *Puce.* – Black, brown, dark olive, dark crimson, dark claret.
- *Dark Blue.* – Black, brown, dark crimson, dark green, dark claret, dark olive, dark blue.
- *Pale Blue.* – Dark crimson, dark green, black, brown, claret, puce, dark blue, dark olive, lavender, orange, yellow.

- *Olive* will dye brown, black, dark green, dark crimson, dark claret.
- *Lavender*. – Black, brown, dark crimson, claret, lavender, olive.
- *Pink*. – Dark crimson, dark green, black, brown, pink, olive, dark blue, dark puce, dark fawn.
- *Rose*. – Same as pink, but also orange, scarlet, and giraffe.
- *Straw, Primrose, and Yellow* will dye almost any colour required, as also will peach and giraffe.
- *Grey* will only dye, besides brown and black, dark green, dark claret, dark crimson, dark fawn, dark blue.
- *White silk* and cotton goods can be dyed almost any colour. White woollen goods cannot be properly dyed in the piece; they can, however, be beautifully cleaned. As cotton, silk, and wool all take dye differently, it is almost impossible to re-dye a fabric of mixed stuff any colour except the dark ones named. Pale blue fabrics will re-dye better than those of any other colour.

SHOES & SOCKS

A Hint on Laces. It is not generally known that bootlaces, if slightly waxed, do not easily come untied. This is a valuable piece of information for those who habitually wear lace boots and shoes. The want of a tag will not be felt if the end of the lace is carefully waxed.

A Tight Shoe may be made sometimes quite easy and comfortable by laying a cloth wet in hot water across where it pinches. This should be changed several times, and the moist heat will cause the leather to *shape itself to the foot*. Many people throw a pair of boots away rather than suffer the discomfort of having their joints or toes pinched.

New Socks. A pair of new socks feel very comfortable to the feet, but the man who wears them before they are washed makes a mistake. Hosiery should always be washed before being worn, as the washing shrinks the threads and makes the socks wear as long again, besides preventing the feet being injured by the colouring. When put on before washing they stretch out of shape and can never be restored to the original form.

Patent Leather should always be warmed to prevent it from cracking, before inserting the foot in the shoe. Heat renders patent leather soft and pliable.

Squeaking Boots. The remedy for these is to boil linseed oil. Pour into a deep dish and place the boots in it, so as to allow the oil to saturate the soles thoroughly for a few days. If this does not remove the annoyance, repeat the process.

To Waterproof Boots and Shoes. Boots and shoes may be rendered permanently waterproof by soaking them for some hours in thick soap-water. A fatty acid is forced in the leather by the soap which makes it impervious to water.

Soles for Boots and Shoes cut from old felt hats are more comfortable than cork, and quite as warm.

When to Try on New Shoes. There is a time for everything in this world, and so it is that the best time to get fitted for shoes is the *latter part of the day*. The feet are then at their maximum size. Activity naturally enlarges them. Much standing tends also to enlarge the feet. New shoes should always be tried on over moderately thick stockings.

Air Your Shoes. No article of attire requires more ventilation than shoes that are worn daily, and none, perhaps, receive less attention in this respect. Excellent hygienic results may be obtained by *applying ammonia* of moderate strength to the inner surface of the soles by means of a small sponge attached to a wire and allowing the shoes to dry. This treatment of the soles will add greatly to the comfort and health of the feet, and should be repeated at least once a fortnight.

STORING CLOTHES PROPERLY

To Pack a Fur Garment in the ordinary manner of packing is *fatal*. A boa may be wonderfully freshened in appearance by shaking it upside down, causing the fur to stand out in that round, fluffy way which makes the boa such a pretty setting for fair faces. Boas should be looped in long loops before hanging that the strain may not rest on any point altogether. If they are ornamented by ribbons they may be hung by these.

When Packing Dresses put paper between the folds to prevent creasing.

White Clothing, if put away in a dark closet or drawer will become yellow. But if it is placed in a box lined with blue paper, or even wrapped in a dark blue cloth, it will come out as white as ever it was, no matter how long it lies. To whiten clothes that have become yellow, steep them overnight in lukewarm water, and next morning wash them in good, clean suds, then put them in the copper, with cold water, and some bits of *curd soap*, and one teaspoonful of powdered borax. Boil for twenty minutes, rinse immediately, and leave them for another night in clean cold water, to which a little powdered borax has been added.

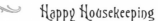
Cupboards should be Aired the same as bedrooms, and the coming architect, if a woman, will see that cupboards in which clothes are hung are provided with a window, be it ever so small. This window will be protected so that in nearly all weathers it may remain open and supply the cupboards with fresh air and light.

To Save Trouble in Packing *always keep a list* either in your trunk or your travelling bag of those things which you will need while you are away from home. Half the labour of packing is saved by knowing exactly what you have to pack, and though your wants will vary a little, still the greater number of them will be the same in spite of seasons, and therefore a list like this will be most useful.

The Printing Ink on Newspapers acts as a deterrent to moths, so woollen goods should be wrapped in them when they are laid by for the summer.

Winter Clothing. It is preferable in winter to wear loose rather than tight clothing, because the loose dress encloses a stratum of warm air which the tight dress shuts out. For the same reason woollen articles, though not warm in themselves keep warm air near to the body.

 WHAT TO DO ON WASHING DAY

To Wash Ribbons. Many ladies are unaware that, with the exception of a few delicate colours – pink, light blue, *&c.* – almost any ribbons can be washed and ironed, and made to look nearly, if not quite, as well as new. To wash ribbons make a clear lather of clean white soap – the water as warm as you can bear your hands in – and rub the ribbons through this. Soap may be applied on the wrong side when there are any grease spots; rinse in cold water. As soon as washed, without hanging out to dry, have ready a hot iron, and press them out while wet; press on the wrong side; they will wrinkle, and never look well, if not pressed while wet. If you wish to stiffen them, dip them before ironing in a solution of gum-arabic. When ironed smooth, take the scissors and trim off the ends.

Stockings should always be turned inside out and well shaken before being washed; they should also be washed by themselves and in different water from any other clothing.

To Clean White Ostrich Feathers. Four ounces of white soap, cut small and dissolve in four pints of warm water; make the solution into a lather by beating. Introduce the feathers, and rub well with the hands for five or six minutes. After this soaping wash them in clean water, as hot as the hands can bear. Shake before the fire until dry.

Embroidery should always be ironed on the wrong side to bring out the design. It should be thoroughly dried.

To Clean Straw Hats. Wash them with soap and water, rinse in clean water, dry in the air, and then wash them over with the white of an egg beaten to a froth. Another method is to rub the straw with cut lemon *dipped in sulphur*, and wash the juice off carefully with water, then stiffen with the white of egg.

Soapsuds should never be wasted. Few persons know how valuable they are when used as manure. Applied to the roots of vines, fruit trees, *&c.,* they impart a vigour and rapidity of growth which is surprising. No one who is lucky enough to have a garden ought to allow soapsuds to be thrown away.

Before Washing Coloured Cottons it is a good plan to put them in four quarts of boiling water, to which has been added three gills of salt. Let them soak in this till the water is cold. This will make the colours fast, and they may be washed safely without fear of fading.

Add a Little Paraffin in the water used for boiling clothes; it will greatly improve their colour.

Clothes-Pegs boiled a few moments and quickly dried, once or twice a month, become more flexible and durable. Clothes-line will last longer and keep in better order if occasionally treated in the same way.

Brown Cotton Stockings should not be ironed, for the frequent application of a hot iron makes them fade and yellow in colour. After being dried they can be smoothed out on the ironing-board with the hands.

When Damping Clothes for ironing the water should be as hot as the hand can bear. It is not necessary to use so much water as it is when the water is cold.

Pillow Slips should be ironed lengthways instead of crosswise, if one wishes to iron wrinkles out instead of in.

Woollen Goods should never be wrung after washing, for this stretches them. They should be put through a wringer and hung out to dry.

 KEEPING YOUR HOME 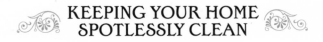 SPOTLESSLY CLEAN

In House Cleaning begin with the attic.

Dusting. Nothing destroys the beauty of the hands like dusting. A pair of housemaid's gloves need not cost one shilling, and will be of great use.

Rings that have valuable stones in them should always be taken off when washing one's hands, as the constant soaping discolours the gems, and also in many cases loosens them from the setting.

To clean a Kettle. Fill it with *potato parings*, and then boil fast till clean.

To Clean Baths. When a scum forms on the inside of a bath, or the stationary marble wash-basins, rub the places with dry salt, and they will come off without any trouble.

If the Handles of Stove Brushes are kept clean from the first, that part of the work will seem no dirtier than any other about the house. It is an excellent plan to use a paint-brush for putting on the blacking, also use plenty of fresh newspapers for polishing.

When Cleaning Plate you will find your efforts greatly assisted by putting your spoons and forks to dry, close to the fire, after you have put on the powder, and if you mix the latter (at any rate occasionally) with *a little gin instead of water*, you will get a better polish. Do not brush off the powder until it is quite dry. Always brush off before using the leather.

Grained Wood can be kept very nice if washed in *cold tea*.

To Clean a Feather Pillow. This can be done without taking out the feathers. Put the pillows into a large tub or bath, and scrub them well with a small brush dipped in a solution of chloride of lime and warm water. Afterwards rinse the pillows thoroughly, spread them on the grass to dry, or on tables in the open air, turning them constantly. After two days of this treatment in a warm, strong sun, pin the pillows on to a clothes-line on every fine or windy day till they are quite dry, then *beat them with a cane*; this will disentangle the feathers, and the pillows will be like new.

To Clean Earthenware or glass quickly, place the articles in salt and water.

Dull, Faded Carpets should be occasionally washed over with warm water to which has been added a little *ammonia*.

To Brighten the Inside of a Teapot. Fill with water, add a small piece of soap, and let it boil about twenty-five minutes.

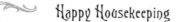

Bedrooms should not be scoured in winter, as colds and sickness may be produced thereby. Dry scouring upon the French plan, which consists of rubbing the floors with dry brushes, may be resorted to, and will be found more effective than would be imagined.

Ceilings that have been smoked by an oil lamp should be washed with soda-water.

Mason's Dust from stone-sawing makes a perfect substance for scouring floors and plain deal tables, rendering them white and beautiful.

To Clean Decanters. Clean decanters with strips of brown paper and cold water, filling the decanter quite full of the paper. Tea-leaves, potato-parings, and shot are also used, but nothing gives the polish of brown paper.

Finger-marks may be removed from varnished furniture by the use of a little sweet oil upon a soft cloth.

Salt and Lemon-Juice will remove iron rust.

Plaster of Paris. Ornaments may be cleaned by covering them with a thick layer of starch, letting it dry thoroughly and then brushing with a stiff brush.

Glasses Wipe to Perfection if washed in very hot water.

Mildew on leather may be removed by gently rubbing with vaseline.

Durable Furniture Polish. Put a quarter of a pint of *turpentine*, a quarter of a pint of *spirits of wine*, and a quarter of a pint of *vinegar* into a bottle, with a third of a pint of linseed oil; cork tightly, and shake the bottle briskly in order to mix the various ingredients thoroughly before using. Dust the furniture carefully, remove any grease spots there may be with a flannel dipped in warm soda-water, then pour a small quantity of the polish on a piece of clean, soft, old flannel, and rub it well into the wood, and polish off at once with a very soft duster – an old silk handkerchief is the best thing for this purpose. If only a small quantity of the polish is used, the furniture will brighten much more easily than when the mixture is laid on thickly.

To Clean Chessmen that are yellow with age and fingering, brush them gently with a firm brush, then make a paste of fine sawdust, damped with water, and a few drops of lemon-juice. Spread this thickly all over the pieces, let it dry thoroughly, and a day or two after brush it all off with the same firm brush. The operation can be repeated if not satisfactory the first time.

Lime and Water, mixed to the consistency of cream, is the best cleanser and brightener of zinc.

Keep Pearls in dry magnesia, starch, or cornflour, instead of in cotton-wool. These stones absorb grease very quickly, and unless kept in something absolutely dry and without the slightest suspicion of grease they rapidly lose the brilliancy which is their chief beauty.

Tiles when Washed should be wiped over with paraffin, which will insure their keeping clean for a very much longer period than if they were merely washed with soap and water.

Paint can be Removed from glass by rubbing it with hot strong vinegar.

Moisture is the Great Enemy of the Piano, and it cannot be too carefully guarded against.

Sweet Oil will improve patent leather. Rub over the surface with a bit of cotton-wool dipped in the oil, and then polish with a soft duster.

Cleaning Diamonds. Wash the stones with soap and water, and dry. Procure some good soft blotting-paper, and with it, folded to a point, clean out all the corners of the settings, polishing the stone at the same time.

To Clean Painted Woodwork. Take two quarts of hot water, two tablespoonfuls of turpentine and one of skimmed milk, and only soap enough to make suds. The mixture will clean and give lustre.

Stone or Marble Hearths should be rubbed with pumice-stone and soap, and rinsed carefully afterwards.

Clean Paint with cold tea, unless it be white, when milk will be found to have a better effect.

Curtain Rings sometimes run with great difficulty and seem to stick to the pole. To remedy this take all the rings off and well rub the pole with paraffin until it is quite smooth, when the rings may be replaced, and will be found to slip along with the greatest ease.

Window Cleaning. This necessary, though unpleasant task, may be much lightened in the following manner: Powder some whiting (calcium carbonate) very finely, and tie it up in a piece of muslin. With this "dab" the glass all over – the dirtier the pane the more whiting will stick to it. Then smear it evenly, all over, with a rag moistened in water, and allow the surface to dry thoroughly. Now rub all off with a chamois leather, and your windows will be beautifully clean, without the usual mess of water, drying-cloths, *&c.*

 RIDDING THE HOME OF DISAGREEABLE SMELLS

Tobacco Smoke Hanging about a Room. To remove the disagreeable smell of stale tobacco smoke in sitting-rooms, open the windows wide as early as possible in the morning.

To Remove the Odour of Paint, slice a few onions and put them in a pail of water in the *centre of the room*; leave it there for several hours; or plunge a handful of hay into a pail of water, and let it stand in the room overnight.

Air should always Circulate freely all round a bed. If placed with one side close to a wall, the sleeper's breath is thrown back, and partly inhaled again, which is injurious.

A Room of Equable Temperature, and well ventilated, goes far to stave off chills and colds, and produces *healthier brains and happier spirits*.

To Purify the Kitchen from unpleasant odours burn vinegar, resin, or sugar.

A Small Piece of Bread put in a clean bit of muslin and put into pots of vegetables while cooking will prevent smells.

Cabbage Water is the cause of disagreeable smells in many houses because the cook will not throw the water away directly she has done with it, nor rinse the pot with clean water. Where possible pour the cabbage water on the earth.

How to Perfume Notepaper. Get a few quires of blotting-paper, and sprinkle each sheet with the perfume required, then put it under a weight until it becomes dry. When dry put the notepaper and envelopes between the sheets, and put them under a weight for a few hours. When removed they will be found perfumed. The blotting-paper sheets may be utilised several times, and can be made to retain their perfume for a long time by keeping them from exposure to the air.

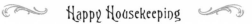

 DECORATING THE HOME

A Room with a Low Ceiling will seem higher if the window curtains hang to the floor.

A Wire Fireguard should belong to each grate in a well-directed household. Their cost is small, and their use is a great safeguard against damage to property and life, especially where wooden logs are burnt. Fireguards should always be placed on before leaving a room.

On Choosing Wall-paper. Almost all green wall-paper is poisonous, as *arsenic* is employed to produce that colour. Some red colours have also a dangerous amount of arsenic.

The Most Restful Colours for the eyes are green and blue. Do not surround yourself with very bright colours. Red is blinding.

To Clean Wall-Paper. Mix four pounds of common flour with two pints of cold water; knead it into a stiff dough, and make it into two or three balls. Wipe the paper all over with it, and as the dough becomes dirty work the soiled part into the middle and the clean outside. This quantity of dough is sufficient to clean a very large room. Begin at the top of the paper and work downwards. This is a never-failing remedy, easy to manage, and will not damage the most delicate paper.

To Remove old Wall-paper. Wet the paper all over two or three times a day with a damp cloth. When the paper is made quite wet in this way it will easily peel off. If the walls are to be repapered, wash them first with soda and water, to which have been added a few drops of carbolic acid. The latter is a strong purifier and disinfectant.

If You want to Paper a Room Yourself buy a plain paper. These are to be had in a variety of plain, beautiful tints, and save no end of trouble in having no pattern to match as each strip is put on. Fancy borders, in colours to match, come about a foot wide, and a much richer effect is gained by using these papers than it is possible to get with the figured kind.

The Benefit of Lamp Shades. Artificial lights hurt the eyesight more or less, but most of all when they are placed on a level with the eyes. A shade of some kind should always be used, which not only protects the eyes from the bright glare but makes the light fall directly on the book or work.

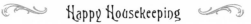

Linoleum is a very good substitute for wood or tiles for a kitchen dado. It is easy to wash, and has a very clean appearance. If liked, it may be varnished occasionally.

In Choosing a Carpet that will have a great deal of hard wear, and that you wish to last well, take one with a small design, as they are generally the best cloth, and also are most suited to patching and turning about without waste of material.

The Unhealthiness of Carpets. The substitution of a central carpet for one covering the whole floor is a great improvement, the floor round the carpet being covered with parquet veneering; or, if the expense is too great, the whole floor may be painted with two good coats of dark oil paint, and varnished, the joints of the boards having first been made secure. The carpet should be made easily removable, in order that it and the floor may be thoroughly cleaned at intervals. Rugs will be found even better, since they may be taken up and shaken every day, if necessary. In bedrooms, the less carpet the better.

To Renew the Colours in a carpet, sponge it with a solution of one part ox-gall to two parts water.

Beat a Carpet on the wrong side first, and then more gently on the right side. Beware of using sticks with sharp points, which may tear the carpet.

Never have a Dark Carpet and Walls in a room that is deficient in light. Only very sunny apartments will stand *gloomy tones* in decoration.

To Stop the Ravages of Moths in Carpets. Camphor will not stop the ravages of moths after they have commenced eating. A good way to kill them is to take a coarse towel, and wring it out in clean water. Spread it smoothly on the carpet, then iron it dry with a hot iron, repeating the operation on all suspected places, and those least used. It does not injure the pile or colour of the carpet in the least; it is not necessary to press hard, heat and steam being the agents, and they do the work effectually on worms and eggs.

To Prepare a Floor for a Dance, it should be swept and scrubbed, and then, when dry, well sprinkled with powdered boracic acid, which should be rubbed in thoroughly. The children of the house may with advantage be allowed to dance on it, or to *slide up and down*, for nothing polishes a floor better than a few pairs of active feet.

Stair Carpets should always have three or four thicknesses of paper put under at the edge of every stair, which is the part where they first wear out.

POINTS OF HOUSEHOLD ECONOMY

When to Buy Candles. Always purchase those made in winter, as they are the best, and buy a good stock of them at once, as they improve if kept for some time in a cool place.

Old Nail-holes may be filled with the following mixture, which is at once simple and effective: Take fine sawdust and mix into a thick paste with glue. Stuff the holes with it, and when dry they will not be noticeable.

If a Pipe has a Leak and drips, the hole may be effectually stopped up until the plumber comes, with a paste made of yellow soap and powdered whiting mixed together with a little water.

On Buying Sheets. Always buy sheets a few inches wider than is necessary to cover the beds, for when the middle of the sheet is becoming thin, it should be cut in two down the centre, the selvedges seamed together, and the sides hemmed. The sheet will then be almost as good as new.

Cotton Sheets are warmer than linen ones.

A String in the Handles of Brooms and Brushes, and nails on the wall to hang them up by, prevents their growing misshapen, and is a very great economy.

Flowers may be kept Fresh overnight if they are excluded entirely from the air. To do this wet them thoroughly, put in a damp box, and cover with wet blotting-paper, then place them in a cool room.

To Keep Irons from Rusting wrap them in *common brown paper* and put away in a dry place. If they have become rusty, they may be made smooth and bright by putting some white sand on a smooth board and rubbing the iron over it several times.

To Preserve a Bouquet. First sprinkle it lightly with fresh water, then put it into a vessel containing *soapsuds*. Take the bouquet out of the suds every morning, and lay it sideways (the stalk entering first) into clean water; keep it there for two minutes, then take it out, and sprinkle the flowers lightly with water. Replace it in the soapsuds, and it will be as fresh as when first gathered. The suds should be changed every three days. If carefully treated in this way, wedding and other bouquets may be kept bright for at least a month.

Pieces of Soap should never be wasted. When they are too small for use they should be put away carefully for washing. They may be cut either in pieces and boiled for washing flannels, or put into the boiler. Small pieces of toilet soap should also be saved. They can be melted up again with a little milk, if necessary, and made into a fresh cake.

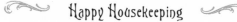

To Economise Coal. Put a few *lumps of chalk* with the coal at the back of the fire. This will give out a good heat and last some time. Coal that is kept in a dry, airy place, will burn much longer than that which is kept in a close cellar with no ventilation. When coal is kept in an airless place it gets rid of its gas, and the absence of this renders it less powerful and more wasteful when burned.

Paper Bags, in which many articles are sent from the grocer's, should be saved for use when blacking a stove. The hand can be slipped into one of these, and the brush handled just as well, and the hands will not be soiled.

Corkscrews are not always at hand when wanted. When this is the case use an *ordinary screw, with a string attached*, to pull out the cork.

Revive Withered Flowers. Plunge the stalks into boiling water, and allow them to remain until the water is cold. By that time the flowers will have revived. Cut off the ends of the stalks, and arrange the flowers in cold water, and they will keep fresh for several days.

When a Sewing-Machine Works Stiffly, put it *near the fire for a few minutes*, so that the working parts of it get warm. This will generally make it work quite easily, but it is sometimes necessary to use a little oil as well.

To prevent Unframed Oil Paintings from sticking together, whether in storing or packing them, proceed as follows: Cut ordinary corks into halves and insert needles into them. Stick these into the corners of the canvas, and by this means the pictures will be kept effectually apart.

To make Glue Waterproof soak it in water until soft, then melt it in linseed oil, assisted by gentle heat. This glue is not acted upon by water or damp.

Old Flannel has almost no end of uses in its capacity as a cleanser. For cleaning of all kinds it is excellent, and for polishing silver it is almost as good as chamois leather.

Economical Use of Nutmegs. If a person begins to grate a nutmeg at the stalk end, it will prove hollow throughout, whereas the same nutmeg grated from the other end would be round and solid to the last.

How to Cool a Room. The simplest and cheapest way to cool a room when the weather is oppressively hot, is to wet a cloth of any size, the larger the better, and suspend it in the place you want to cool. Let the room be well ventilated, and the temperature will sink as much as twelve degrees in less than an hour. This is a plan adopted by many Eastern nations.

Dishcloths may be knitted on coarse wooden needles of the string which is tied round tradesmen's parcels. They are strong and have a rough surface, and are capital for cleaning. They should be boiled in soda-water to keep them sweet.

To Begin a Fire. If a coal fire is low *throw on a little sugar*, and it will brighten at once.

How to Take Creases out of Paper. The creases may be taken out of papers intended for binding by sprinkling them with water, throwing it on with a whisk broom, then putting the papers under heavy weights until dry. A crease in a picture may be damped then covered with a cloth and ironed.

To Absorb Damp in a Cupboard. Fill a small box with lime, and place upon a shelf. This will result in the air in the cupboard being kept both dry and sweet.

When putting away the Silver Tea- or Coffee-Pot which is not used every day, lay a little stick across on the top under the cover. This will allow the fresh air to get in, and prevent mustiness.

The Best Way to Mend Torn Pages of Books is to paste them with tissue-paper—the print will show through it.

Steel Pens are destroyed by the acid in the ink. If an old nail, or steel pen is put in the ink, the acid will exhaust itself on them, and pens in daily use will last much longer.

A Hammock will prove a Boon to a person who has grown weary of bed. It can be strung across a room from the door frame to a window-casing, and may be hung over the bed, where the patient can slip into it at will.

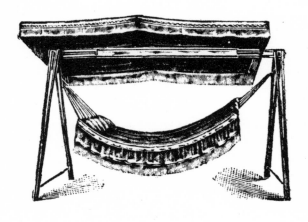

Hot-water Cans and Jugs made of Tin will last very much longer if turned upside down directly they are emptied, it is the few drops remaining at the bottom which cause rust and make tiny holes.

Burst Pipes in Frosty Weather. When this occurs in a house it is a most unpleasant experience, so I would remind my readers that if taps are kept turned so that they will just drip, and a lamp stood near them at night, it will prevent the water from freezing.

ITEMS FOR THE KITCHEN CUPBOARD

Soda one of the Most Useful Household Necessaries. A little added to water in which greasy dishes are washed to a great extent destroys the grease, and keeps the dishcloth in good condition. For scouring all wooden articles it may be used with advantage.

No Kitchen should be without Scales, to test the integrity of things purchased by weight, and to measure the given quantities of the various recipes.

Charcoal is a great *air-purifier*. In the case of a damp and badly ventilated cellar, a few trays of charcoal placed about it will soon dry and sweeten the air.

Blacklead is an Excellent Lubricator. Try the tip of a lead pencil on a squeaking door-hinge, and see the result.

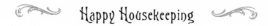

A Spatula or Palette Knife is the best thing for scraping butter or porridge, *&c.,* from the sides of bowls or pots; it is not expensive and soon saves its cost by preventing waste.

Turpentine in the Home. After a housekeeper fully realises the worth of turpentine in the household she is never willing to be without a supply of it. It gives *quick relief to burns*; it is an excellent application for *corns*; it is good for *rheumatism and sore throats*. It is a sure preventive against moths; by just dropping a trifle in the drawers, chests, and cupboards, it will render the garments secure from injury during the summer. It will *keep ants from the closets* and store-rooms by putting a few drops in the corners and upon the shelves; it is sure *destruction to bed-bugs*, and will effectually drive them away from their haunts if thoroughly applied to all the joints of the bedstead, and injures neither furniture nor clothing. A spoonful added to a pail of warm water is excellent for *cleaning paint*.

Glycerine is very slow to freeze, and if a little is put on taps in frosty weather, and exposed pipes are covered with pieces of old carpet or sacking, the water is not likely to freeze.

PERFECTING PEST CONTROL

To Destroy Beetles. Make wafers with *red lead*, flour, and water, rolled out thin, then put on to a baking-sheet to dry. These wafers are *very poisonous*, so must not be within the reach of children and animals.

Mice greatly dislike camphor, so if put into places they frequent it will drive them away completely.

A Cure for a Flea Pest. Place the common adhesive fly-paper on the floors of the rooms infested, with *a small piece of fresh meat* in the centre of each sheet; it will be found that the fleas will jump towards the meat and adhere to the paper.

Flies may be prevented from settling on picture-frames and furniture by soaking a large bundle of leeks for five or six days in a pail of water, and then washing the pictures, *&c.*, with it.

Rats hate chloride of lime, and avoid places where it is exposed.

Worms in Pot Plants. Water the plant with lime-water, which will bring them to the surface.

Cockroaches may be destroyed by mixing and placing in their way at night two ounces of powdered borax, one ounce of *sugar of lead*, and three ounces of wheat-flour.

Common Salt used freely will entirely exterminate snails. A ring of salt placed round articles will prevent snails disturbing them.

Carbolic Soap not only keeps mosquitoes off, but every kind of insect, for which reason it is wise to *use it to scrub floors and paint*; one should always take a cake when travelling.

STAINS – AND HOW TO ERADICATE THEM

Tea Stains on China Cups are often an accepted evil with housekeepers. They are usually removable, however, with salt and water and vigorous rubbing. A particularly obstinate case may be treated with *bone dust and water*, the bone dust being obtainable from any druggist.

Mildewed Articles soaked in *sour milk* will remove all traces of stains.

To Remove Wine Stains. Hold the stained article in milk that is boiling on the fire till the stains have boiled out.

150

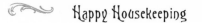

When washing any cloth stained with egg, avoid putting it in boiling water, which will set the stain till it is almost permanent. Soak the cloth first in cold water, and the stain may easily be removed. The same rule applies to egg-cups and any dishes stained with egg. If they are thrown with the other china, into hot soda-water, the stain hardens on the plate or glass, and it requires considerable patience to remove it; but it comes off easily in cold water.

Ink-Stains on Books may be removed by oxalic acid. It should be diluted with water, applied with a small paint-brush, and then dabbed with blotting-paper. More than one application may be necessary.

To Remove Bloodstains. The following is a good way to remove bloodstains, which can otherwise be difficult to get out: Make a thin paste of starch and water; spread over the stain. When dry, brush the starch off, and the stain is gone. Two or three applications will remove the worst stains.

To Extract Ink-stains from Wood, scour with sand wet with ammonia. Rinse with strong soda-water.

To Remove Grease from Leather apply the white of an egg to the spot and dry in the sun.

Ripe Tomatoes will remove ink stains from white cloth, also stains from the hands.

When Tea is Spilt on a White Tablecloth pour boiling water through the stains immediately. This will prevent their spreading, and render them easier to remove when the cloth is washed.

Lamp Oil well rubbed in will remove the white spots on tables caused by hot plates.

Yellow Piano Keys may be made white by rubbing them gently with sandpaper and polishing with a chamois leather.

Leather that has Become Dull and shabby-looking may be very much improved in appearance by being *rubbed over with the white of an egg* well beaten.

THE FOLDING OF FANCY SERVIETTES.

No. I. — The "Mirette."

In serviette folding there are three essentials to success: a perfect square, a certain amount of stiffness, and careful creasing of the various folds. It is important, then, that one's table linen should not only be carefully hemmed, but properly ironed, the two opposite edges being smoothed first, the remaining two next, and lastly the centre. With regard to stiffness, this varies slightly with the different methods of folding, some modes requiring much more rigidity than others. While admitting that starch is a decided improvement to table linen, many people are of the opinion that it renders the serviettes harsh for use. That undoubtedly is true, but for special table decoration at least, it is surely worth putting up with that *slight discomfort* for the sake of *effect*.

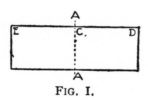

FIG. I.

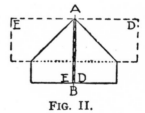

FIG. II.

The "Mirette" is a fairly simple style. Undo a moderately stiff serviette till it is merely folded across in three, as in Fig. I (the laundress should always treat it thus before folding it into squares).

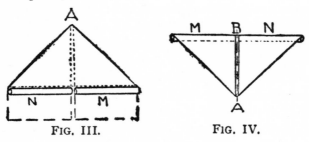

FIG. III.   FIG. IV.

Then fold the edges C–E and C–D (Fig. I) down till they meet the centre A–B (Fig. I) as shown in Fig. II. There will then be a triangle, with two ends overlapping. Roll these ends up till they are level with the base of the triangle, as in Fig. III. Now turn the whole over, so that the rolls are underneath (as shown by dotted lines in Fig. IV), and the point A is nearest to you instead of the rolls M and N.

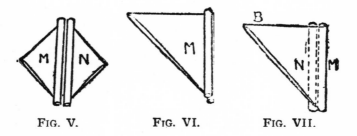

FIG. V.   FIG. VI.   FIG. VII.

Then bring the rolls M and N to the centre A–B, so that they lie side by side, as shown in Fig. V. The next part requires to be carefully followed. Take the rolls in the right hand, so that the roll M is on the top of N as you lay it down on its side, when a triangular piece will flap out on the left, as shown in Fig. VI. Slightly shift the rolls, so as to place them side by side, with M on the right and N on the left, as in Fig. VII.

FIG. VIII.

Now take hold of the corner B, and bring it to the base of the centre between the rolls. The three-cornered piece will then form a conical fold, into which bread should be slipped to keep it in place as illustrated in Fig. VIII.

No. II.—The "Duchess"

A decidedly stiff serviette will be required for the method of folding treated in this article. It is for insertion in a wine-glass. Take a square serviette and open it out flat. Then fold it across line D (Fig. I.) so that corner A is on the same level as corner B. Next make a crease level with the points C, fold down corner A (Fig II.).

FIG. I.

Turn over and repeat the process with corner B, folding level with same part as A (Fig. II.), and your serviette should be as represented in Fig. III. Before proceeding further, next glance at Fig. V., which will prove of material assistance, showing as it does what the serviette ought to look like at the end of the next stage, for which the ensuing directions should be followed:

FIG. II.

FIG. III.

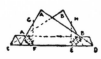

FIG. IV.

156

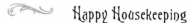
On reference to Fig. IV., on the right side, you will see an edge marked E–D. Fold this up so that it rests on the line E–H, with point D resting on point H.

FIG. V.

To do this you will find it necessary to fold the point up across the line E–B. Edge F–C should be similarly treated, so that it rests on line F–G, and in that case you will have to make a fold across A–F. Having done this your serviette should be as represented in Fig. V., after it has been pleated up evenly, so that the pleats run from top to bottom. The base is then inserted in a wine-glass, and Fig. VI. will convince you that you have an ornament to any dinner or luncheon table.

The method shown in this article is as effective as it is simple. Moreover, it lends a "spikiness" to the appearance of the table, which is much to be desired. Every alternate serviette might be folded in this manner, those intervening being made up in one of the flatter styles. It is unnecessary to remark that a limp serviette would be useless here, for the "Duchess" requires the stiffest of napery, and it would be well to slightly starch serviettes which have seen much wear if they are to be treated in this way.

FIG. VI.

No. III.—The "Water Lily"

Open out the serviette, and see that it is perfectly square, for if not no good result can be obtained. It is also important that the serviette be very stiff, otherwise it will flop, and take a lot of room on the table instead of standing up.

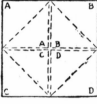

FIG. I.

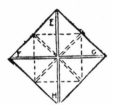

FIG. II.

Commence by folding all four corners to the centre, as in Fig. I., which shows the original square, and dotted lines indicating the position of the corners after folding, hence the double sets of A, B, C, and D. Again fold the four corners E, F, G, and H, to the centre, as shown in Fig. II. The dotted lines in Fig. II. merely show the position of the edges underneath.

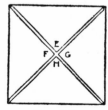

FIG. III.

Fig. III. is a representation of the serviette at the same stage, but without the dotted lines, so is perhaps less confusing. Now turn the serviette over, so handling it that you keep it from becoming disarranged. To effect this it will be found necessary to place a finger of each hand, one on the upper and one on the under side of the centre. Fold the four corners I, J, K, and L (Fig. IV.) to the centre, in the position indicated by the dotted lines. Having done this, your serviette should appear as Fig. V. Now place the forefinger of your left hand in the centre, and feel underneath for a point in a straight line with point W (Fig. VI.) and the centre.

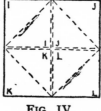

FIG. IV.

FIG. V.

With the thumb and forefinger of the right hand pull this out sharply in an upward direction, keeping a firm hold of the centre, as previously directed, that the whole serviette may not come unfolded. Feel underneath again for three other points, between corners X, Y, Z, and the centre, and pull these out in a similar way, keeping the forefinger of the left hand firmly in the centre of the serviette all the while. You have now four points pulled out, each similar to W on Fig. VI. Still keep a firm hold of the centre, and again feel underneath with the right hand, and you will find four other points, which should be pulled outward and upward, and when in position will be found to be alternate with the four first points pulled out.

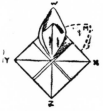

Fig. VI.

Fig. VII. shows how the serviette will look when this has been done and a small tumbler has been placed in the centre.

Fig. VII.

This mode of folding is so straightforward that it is well-nigh impossible to handle the serviette wrongly, but it will be found that unless a well-starched one be used, the "Water Lily" will be flat, and unlike the beautiful flower it represents, instead of being cup-like in shape, and fitting closely round the tumbler placed in the centre.

No. IV.—"The Peacock"

One only needs to glance at Fig. IV. to understand that a very stiff serviette is necessary to successfully carry out this design. Two of them are used, one forming the head, neck, and tail, and the other the ruff.

To form the head, &c., take a good stiff serviette and open it out square, then crease it across B–C (Fig. I.). Next pleat the part below this line, so that the pleats run perpendicularly, as shown in Fig. I.

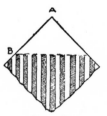

FIG. I

The top corner A (Fig. I.) is then either taken between the teeth, or fixed firmly with a pin on to a table of convenient height; of the two, placing it between the teeth will probably answer best, for the edges A–B and A–C have next to be rolled to the centre, and one is able to get at them better if the top corner be held in the teeth. You will then have the top part of your serviette rolled to form the head and neck of the "peacock," and the lower portion pleated to form the tail, as indicated in Fig. II. Insert the part of the serviette where the rolls meet the pleats in a wine-glass, tucking it in firmly. A good deal of the "tail" will have

FIG. II.

become rolled in, and this must be pulled out to the best advantage. It is not possible to give explicit directions for the forming of the head and neck, the rolled part of the serviette being bent to imitate the desired graceful arch of it as nearly as possible.

Do what one will, the immediate end with which the head is to be formed tends decidedly to point upwards, but if a *tiny piece of bread* about the size of a button be inserted in the folds at the end it helps to balance it, and the head is much more easily formed. Moreover, the bread is entirely concealed in the folds, and so is not noticed.

Another serviette is now necessary to form the ruff—for such is its proper name. For this, the napkin should be folded in half down the centre, and the edges folded back again till they are level with the centre fold, and one on either side of it; in other words, the square is folded into four lengthwise, and at the upper edge A–B (Fig. III.) you have a fold in the centre, and a single edge above and below it.

FIG. III.

By careful reference to the end on the left of Fig. III., and comparison with your serviette, you will soon be able to ascertain that you have this point right. The whole is then pleated perpendicularly, as shown in Fig. III. Now take the top edge A–B (Fig. III.) at the top edge of one of the perpendicular pleats which go in, for in the pleating there are naturally some edges which go in and some which stand out. Fold this point down, and repeat the process with every similar point along the top thickness of the edge A–B (Fig. II.).

FIG. IV.

By experimenting with a piece of stiff paper unnecessary handling of the serviette will be avoided – an important point, for its fresh appearance must be preserved. Now turn the serviette over, being careful to keep edge A–B (Fig. III.) farthest from you, and again, taking only the inner points of the top thickness, treat them similarly. You have still along the edge A–B (Fig. III.) a plain fold in the centre. Insert a pencil in this and ruck the fold over it, so as to give the frilly effect, shown in the. ruff of Fig. IV. Close up the pleats at the bottom edge C–D (Fig. III.) and insert this in the same glass as the other serviette, so that the ruff goes crossways between the head and tail.

No. V.—The "Fleur De Lis"

Open out the serviette square, then fold it across from corner to corner, A–E, so that C rests on C (Fig. I.). Fig. II. is an exact representation of it at this stage.

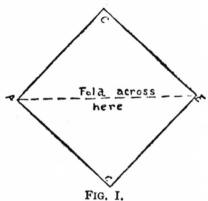

FIG. I.

The edges C–B and A–C are then folded, as shown in Fig. II., to the centre, so that the points A and B meet on D. The lower corner D (Fig. III.) is then folded up till it rests on C. To do this it will be necessary to make a fold across E–F (Fig. III.), as indicated.

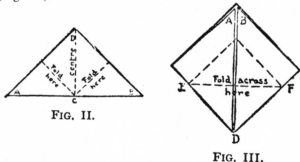

FIG. II.

FIG. III.

Fig. IV. shows how the serviette should now look.

The corner D (Fig. IV.) is then folded down to the base, so that it rests on the other D (Fig. IV.), folding it down across G–H (Fig. IV.), so that the serviette appears as per Fig. V.

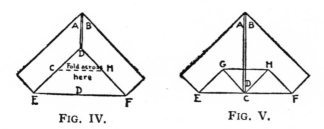

FIG. IV. FIG. V.

Turn it over so that all the edges are underneath, as shown by dotted lines in Fig. VI. The end C–C should be taken in the left hand, and the end E–E in the right. They are then brought together, and one tucked into the other, so that they will remain in that position, and the serviette stand on its own base.

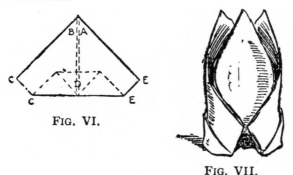

FIG. VI.

FIG. VII.

This is the back of the lily, and it should be in accordance with Fig. VII., the only difference being that the points may be a little less evident. Turn the serviette round, so that the front is towards you, and pull the points A and B (Fig. VIII.) down, so that one droops over on either side, and Fig. IX. shows exactly how your serviette should look when finished.

FIG. VIII.

FIG. IX.

Just a word of reminder to the effect that Fig. VIII. shows the back, and NOT the front view, the roll of bread being placed in the hollow part underneath it. Fig. IX. shows the side points pulled over considerably, but that is, of course, a matter of personal taste, some people preferring them almost erect, as in the case of Fig. VIII., although a resemblance to the lily is then much less noticeable.

 **BIBLIOGRAPHY**

Chambers's Cookery for Young Housewives
(W & R Chambers Ltd, 1890)

Enquire Within Upon Everything (Houlston & Sons, 1890)

*Good Things Made, Said and Done for Every Home and
Household* (Goodall, Backhouse & Co, 1884)

The Lady's Dressing Room (Cassell & Co, 1892)

The Little Folks' Handy Book (Charles Scribner's Sons, 1910)

Things A Woman Wants to Know (C. A. Pearson Ltd, 1901)

THINGS MARRIED WOMEN WANT TO KNOW

1. How to Economise in Housekeeping?

ONE ANSWER IS:

Buy an Alexander Meat Chopper!

It will enable you to vary the weekly Menu by introducing delicious Dishes prepared from Cold Meat, Fish, etc.

It will enable you to use up Cold Joints to the very last scrap of meat, without waste.

It will pay for its own cost in "no time."

Price from 5/- upwards according to size.

A Cookery Book given gratis with each Machine.

2. How to Cook for Invalids?

THE ANSWER IS AGAIN

Buy an Alexander Meat Chopper!

Thousands of Invalids, *all the world over,* know to-day the value of the Alexander Meat Chopper in Invalid Cookery. The Alexander Cookery Book tells you how to prepare Dishes for Invalids with the help of the Meat Chopper.

For people with weak digestion the Alexander Meat Chopper renders capital service **as a Masticator.**

As a Masticator strongly Nickel-plated and polished.

3. How to Feed Invalids and Convalescents who cannot take Solid Food?

Buy an Alexander Meat Juice Extractor, and prepare your own Meat Juice!

The pure juice of Fresh Beef is the finest Meat Extract the world knows, and has most marvellous effect in restoring strength after long illness.

The Medical Adviser should be consulted as to quantity to be given, etc.

To be obtained from all Ironmongers, Stores, etc.

THE ALEXANDER MFG. CO., 42, MOOR LANE, LONDON, E.C.

FAT FOLK

SUFFERING WOMEN

may be relieved from much misery and made strong and active again by taking a course of Bile Beans. During the winter weather many women suffer from a feeling of weakness and chill, bad headaches, and a sensation of depression which makes the days seem long and weary. This state is generally caused by a sluggish state of the blood and liver. In order to restore these organs to their proper condition it is necessary for the digestive organs to be so toned up and strengthened that the food taken is turned into pure, rich blood. The liver should be stimulated to enable it to carry out its various functions and the kidneys put into proper order. Bile Beans act upon all these organs in such a highly beneficial manner that they are speedily restored to their healthy state. The Beans **help** the organs **to do the work**; they do not force them into strained and unnatural condition, so that when the Beans are no longer taken the condition of the patient is worse than before. They are purely vegetable, mild in their action, and particularly suited to the requirements of women.

Bile Beans are unequalled as a remedy for Headache, Indigestion, Constipation, Rheumatism, Liver Chill, Piles, Influenza, Gout, and Liver and Kidney Ailments.

You may obtain them from any chemist, or post free from the Bile Bean Manufacturing Co., 210 and 211 Worship St., London, E.C., upon receipt of prices, 1½d. or 2/9 (the latter size contains three times the quantity). Bile Beans are sold in boxes only—never loose. Avoid worthless imitations.

A FREE SAMPLE.

The Proprietors have so much faith in the efficacy of Bile Beans that they will forward a Sample free, and a Book on Liver and Digestive Ailments, if you send your name and address, and a penny stamp (to cover return postage), along with the accompanying Coupon to the Bile Bean Manufacturing Co.'s Central Distributing Depot, Greek St., Leeds.

BILE BEANS FOR BILIOUSNESS

When you are fagged and thirsty

you'll best appreciate the extraordinary refreshment of

ROSS'S *Belfast Dry Ginger Ale*

Cooling, vivifying, gratifying to the palate and the whole system —not only because of the famous Ross Artesian Well Water, but also because of the choice ingredients and the perfect preparation, which renders bacterial or metallic contamination impossible.

If you feel you need a stronger drink, "Ross" blends and mellows perfectly with whisky, brandy or gin.

Ross's Soda Water has the same natural blending excellence. 2

W. A. ROSS & SONS, Ltd., Belfast.

London : 6, Colonial Avenue, Minories, E. } *(Wholesale only.)*
Glasgow : 38, York Street